Rx for Ailing House Plants

Books by Charles M. Evans with Roberta Lee Pliner

The Terrarium Book
Rx for Ailing House Plants

FOR AILING HOUSE PLANTS

Charles M. Evans

with Roberta Lee Pliner

Random House New York

Drawings by Marika Lutz and Bill Goldsmith

Copyright © 1974 by Charles M. Evans and Roberta Lee Pliner

All rights reserved under International and Pan-American Copyright Conventions. Published in the United States by Random House, Inc., New York, and simultaneously in Canada by Random House of Canada Limited, Toronto.

Library of Congress Cataloging in Publication Data
Evans, Charles M.
Rx for ailing house plants.
1. House plants—Diseases and pests. I. Pliner, Roberta Lee, joint author.
II. Title.
SB608.H84E9   636.9′ 65   73-20566
ISBN 0-394-48683-8
ISBN 0-394-70645-5 (pbk.)

Manufactured in the United States of America
98765432
First Edition

Contents

Rx for Ailing House Plants

Chapter 1

Diagnosing the Ailment

Many indoor plants sometimes suffer from disease or damage caused by insects or the environment, or from physical damage or just plain neglect. It is the rare gardener who has not despaired over some valuable and once beautiful plants that have suddenly become unhealthy and unattractive in spite of receiving the same, apparently adequate routine care that had kept them in peak condition for months or years.

Some plants are certainly more temperamental than others, but with careful attention to their cultural requirements even these can be grown successfully. But it is also true that even the sturdy old stand-by plants—those that seem to grow anywhere—can be afflicted in a variety of ways. Practically any problem, however, can be easily identified and cured by the observant and knowledgeable indoor gardener.

A plant's appearance and growing habits indicate the state **symptoms** of its health. In the early stages of an ailment, signs of ill health are usually relatively subtle: tiny cobwebs in leaf axes, one or two fallen leaves, or faded foliage color. Unchecked, most plant ailments eventually produce rather dramatic symptoms, such as severe defoliation or total withering. But no matter what the particular symptom, the symptom is a clue to the the ailment; it is not the ailment itself.

The following Symptoms and Causes table shows the primary symptoms of various plant ailments: those symptoms which are most easily and frequently noticed and which represent in most cases the first stage of any ailment. Thus, if a particular plant seems to be shedding its foliage more rapidly than usual or its flower buds fail to open, look for these symptoms in this table to determine the possible cause.

Some symptoms, such as yellowing leaves, are caused by several different afflictions; you will have to evaluate that symptom within the context of other symptoms to determine the right cause. For example, a few yellowing leaves, especially if they are older leaves and/or bottom leaves, may reflect nothing more significant than the natural processes of attrition. While the aging process varies from plant to plant, all plants eventually shed their oldest leaves, which frequently turn yellow before dropping off. But, if the yellow color appears mainly along the leaf veins and new growth seems weak or stunted, the cause might be inadequate fertilizing. Or if the entire leaf is spotted yellow and is covered with fine cobwebs, the cause is definitely a mite invasion.

Certain drastic symptoms, such as severe wilting or complete defoliation, are given in the table as the primary symptoms of several cultural or environmental problems. These might also be secondary symptoms representing the most advanced stages of many parasitic invasions. If, in such an instance, none of the causes listed for a particular symptom seem to apply, examine the plant again for additional primary symptoms. In the event of an insect invasion, the primary symptom might be the presence of the insect itself, whereas a disease might first show up as one of several kinds of leaf spots.

Once you think you have found the cause of your plant's **causes** affliction, cross-check the plant in the second table, Plant Problems. Here your diagnosis might be further strengthened by finding that the plant in question is indeed often subject to this particular problem.

The next four chapters give details of each plant problem, preventive measures, chemical and nonchemical remedies, and names of plants most often affected by particular problems. Chapter 2 discusses cultural and environmental difficulties; Chapter 3, nutritional deficiencies; Chapter 4, different types of insect invasions; and Chapter 5, problems resulting from plant diseases.

In Chapters 2 through 5, wherever it is suggested that one ailment might provoke another ailment—such as excessive humidity resulting in fungal diseases—read about the secondary ailment. Treatment of the primary ailment might prevent the development of the secondary ailment. Should you have to treat the plant for two different problems, one remedy might serve to solve both.

Preventive measures, nonchemical controls, chemical controls and recommended formulations, methods of application, and safety cautions are described in Chapter 6. For most plant problems, several different remedies are suggested, but whichever you choose, be sure it is specific to that problem. Applying the wrong therapy to any plant problem is not only wasteful, but if the remedy is a strong one the plant might not survive still another assault on its already weakened structure.

Symptoms	Causes
Leaves	
Curled leaves, dropping off of leaves	Thrips, overwatering, too cool temperatures, drafts
Black coating on leaves	Mildews and molds (diseases)
Leaf spots, dry and depressed	Anthracnose disease
Leaf spots, moist and blistered	Leaf spot disease
Leaf spots, crisp and brown	Underwatering, overfertilizing, air pollution
Leaf spots or blotches, yellow	Mites, scale, leaf spot disease, air pollution, incorrect fertilizing
White, feltlike coating on leaves	Mildews and molds (diseases), mealy bugs
Tips of leaves and/or leaf margins turn brown, die back	Anthracnose disease, overwatering, too low light, too warm temperatures, air pollution, too low humidity, salt damage
Yellow along veins of leaves	Underfertilizing or incorrect fertilizing, too alkaline soil
Soft black/brown areas on leaves	Overwatering, excess humidity
Older leaves drop	Underwatering, too low light, underfertilizing, compacted soil, needs repotting, too warm temperatures

All leaves drop	Underwatering, air pollution, too low light
New leaves soft and discolored	Air pollution, overwatering
Grayish cast to leaves	Too much light
Sticky substance on leaves	Aphids, mealy bugs, scale, white fly
Holes and cuts in leaves	Slugs, physical damage, caterpillars, cockroaches, springtails
Corky scales or protrusions on undersides of leaves	Overwatering
Paling, bleached leaves	Mites, too much or too little light, too little fertilizer, air pollution, underwatering
Winding trails in leaves	Leaf miners
Thick, dwarfed leaves	Salt damage
Papery scars on leaves	Thrips
Leaves rolled inward at tips	Leaf rollers
Chewed leaves	Animals, caterpillars, cockroaches, earwigs, millipedes
Soft, rotted leaf tissue	Overwatering, too high humidity

Flowers

Flower buds drop	Low humidity, too little water, too low light, mites, thrips, white fly, bulb pests
Flowers do not last	Underwatering, too high temperatures

Flowers lack color intensity	Too low light
No flowers (on flowering plants)	Too low light, improper daylength, bulb pests, thrips, too much or too little fertilizer
Flowers deformed, discolored	Thrips, bulb pests

Roots, crowns, stems, and branches

Soft, mushy (rotted) tissue	Crown and stem rot disease, overwatering, excess humidity, too high or low temperatures
Mildews and molds	Mildews and molds (diseases)
Galls on roots	Nematodes
Wilt	Overwatering, poor drainage, underwatering, too much light, too high temperatures, overfertilization, compacted soil, air pollution, too low humidity, needs repotting
Stems weak and limp	Underfertilizing, underwatering
General lack of vigor	Underwatering, too low light, underfertilizing, compacted soil, air pollution
Slow growth	Too low light, too cool or too warm temperatures, compacted soil pH factor, improper daylength, needs repotting

Root deterioration	Nematodes, root rot disease, overwatering, overfertilization, salt damage, pH factor, earthworms, fungus gnats, centipedes, poor drainage, poor repotting, underwatering

Seedlings and new growth

Seedlings collapse	Damping-off disease, too low light
New growth chewed	Slugs, cockroaches
New growth stunted, distorted or weak	Too low light, underfertilizing, too low humidity, needs repotting
Seedlings chewed or cut-off at soil line	Caterpillars and cutworms, ants

Soil and pots

Soil waterlogged	Overwatering, poor drainage
Soil dry, hard-packed	Compacted soil, underwatering
Crusty white on rims of pots, or top of soil	Salt damage

Presence of insects

Brown, hard disks	Scale
Brown or black flying insects	Fungus gnats

Cottony white fluff	Mealy bugs
Jumping organisms in soil	Springtails
Spider webs	Mites
White flying insects	White fly
Specks of excrement	Caterpillars and cutworms, leaf miners, thrips
Shiny, slimy trails on smooth leaves, pots, saucers	Slugs
Tan sesame seed-like particles on undersides of leaves	White fly

Plant Problems

ACUBA	Mites
AFRICAN VIOLETS	Overwatering, root rot disease, leaf spot disease, leaf miners, mealy bugs, mites, nematodes, crown and stem rot
AGLAONEMA	Mealy bugs, crown and stem rot disease, too cool temperatures, overwatering
ALOE	Root rot disease
AMARYLLIS	pH factor, overwatering, bulb pests
ANTHURIUM	Mites, too low humidity
APHELANDRA	Underwatering
ARALIA	Aphids, mites, scale, thrips
ARDISIA	Mites, scale
ASPARAGUS FERN	pH factor
ASPIDISTRA	Mites, scale
AVOCADO	Scale, thrips
AZALEAS	Leaf miners, thrips, white fly, pH factor, underwatering
BEGONIAS	Leaf rollers, thrips, crown and stem rot disease, overwatering, root rot disease
BROMELIADS	Scale, too cool temperatures
BROWALLIA	Leaf miners, white fly
BOUGAINVILLAEA	pH factor
CACTI	Mealy bugs, scale, sowbugs, crown and stem rot disease, leaf spot disease, root rot disease, overwatering, slugs and snails

CALADIUM	Too low humidity, too cool temperatures
CAMELLIA	Scale, pH factor
CHRYSANTHEMUM	Aphids, thrips, white fly
CISSUS	Mealy bugs, mites, underwatering
CITRUS	Aphids, mealy bugs, mites, nematodes, scale, thrips, white fly, anthracnose disease, pH factor
COFFEE PLANT	White fly
COLEUS	Mealy bugs, white fly
COLUMNEA	Overwatering, root rot disease, leaf spot disease, leaf miners, mealy bugs, mites, nematodes, crown and stem rot
CORDYLINE	Mites, overwatering
CRASSULA	Nematodes
CROTON	Mites
CYCLAMEN	Aphids, mites, thrips
DIEFFENBACHIA	Mealy bugs, mites, crown and stem rot disease, too cool temperatures
DIZYGOTHECA	Mealy bugs, mites, overwatering
DRACAENA	Mealy bugs, mites, leaf spot disease, overwatering
EPISCIA	Overwatering, root rot disease, leaf spot disease, leaf miners, mealy bugs, mites, nematodes, crown and stem rot
EUONYMUS	Scale
FATSIA	Aphids, mites
FERNS	Aphids, mealy bugs, scale, thrips, white fly, underwatering, too low humidity

FICUS	Mealy bugs, mites, scale, thrips, anthracnose disease, mildew
FITTONIA	Overwatering, root rot disease, leaf spot disease, leaf miners, mealy bugs, mites, nematodes, crown and stem rot
FLAME VIOLET	Too low humidity
FUCHSIA	Aphids, thrips, white fly
GARDENIA	Aphids, mealy bugs, mites, nematodes, scale, underwatering, pH factor
GERANIUMS	Leaf rollers, white fly, crown and stem rot disease, leaf spot disease, overwatering
GESNERIADS	Root rot disease, overwatering, leaf miners, mealy bugs, mites, nematodes, crown and stem rot disease
GYNURA	Aphids
HERBS	Mealy bugs, mites, white fly
HIBISCUS	Aphids, mealy bugs, mites, scale, white fly
HOLLY	pH factor
HOYA	Mealy bugs, nematodes
IRESINE	Too low humidity
IVY	Aphids, mites, scale, underwatering, too low humidity, too high temperatures
JESSAMINE	Scale
JERUSALEM CHERRY	Scale, thrips, white fly
KALANCHOE	Anthracnose
LANTANA	White fly
LIGUSTRUM	Scale, leaf spot disease

LILIES	pH factor
LOQUAT	pH factor
MARANTA	Mites, humidity, too cool temperatures
MYRTLE	Scale, thrips
OLEANDER	Leaf rollers, scale, anthracnose disease
PALMS	Mealy bugs, mites, scale, anthracnose disease, root rot disease, pH factor
PEPEROMIAS	Overwatering
PHILODENDRON	Mites, crown and stem rots, too cool temperatures
PICK-A-BACK	White fly
PILEAS	Overwatering
PITTOSPORUM	Mealy bugs, scale, heat
POINSETTIA	Mites
PODOCARPUS	Mealy bugs, mites, nematodes, scale, pH factor, too high temperatures
POMEGRANATE	Scale, white fly
ROSES	Mites, leaf rollers, thrips, leaf spot disease, too high humidity
SEA GRAPE	pH factor
SCHEFFLERA	Mealy bugs, mites, scale, overwatering
SELAGINELLA	Too low humidity
SHRIMP PLANT	pH factor
STREPTOCARPUS	Too low humidity
SUCCULENTS	Root rot disease, mealy bugs, crown and stem rot disease, leaf spot disease, overwatering, slugs and snails, sowbugs

SYNGONIUM	Mites
TOMATOES	White fly, underwatering
ZAMIA	Scale

Chapter 2

Cultural and Environmental Problems

When plants are taken from their native habitats and grown indoors, they are frequently subjected to such adverse growing conditions as low light, poor ventilation, high temperature, dry air with a corresponding lack of humidity, and limited drainage and air circulation around their roots. Subsequent growth is weakened or retarded, and incipient disease and insect parasites develop and spread quickly.

Plants that usually grow well indoors are either those whose native habitats happen to resemble the average indoor growing environment or those that adapt well to indoor conditions. These are the plants—and there are many varieties of them—that form the foundation for any plant collection. However, the indoor gardener can successfully cultivate many more delicate plants by adjusting indoor conditions to emulate native environments as closely as possible.

Some of the shrubby flowering evergreens, such as azaleas and jasmine, that are ordinarily cultivated as outdoor plants, require especially favorable indoor growing conditions such as high humidity, a low daytime temperature with a drop of 10 to 20 degrees at night, and extremely good light. Seasonal plants, such as Easter lilies, poinsettias, and spring bulbs, are forced for one-season indoor bloom in practically any growing conditions, but once the plant stops blooming, discard it. It does not suffer from any ailment but rather has reached the end of its life cycle. But even seasonal plants often remain in bloom longer if they are kept in the cool, humid growing conditions that they enjoy outdoors.

The following are cultural and environmental problems that, in some cases, can afflict any plant, and in others, are harmful only to certain varieties of plants.

If the soil composition is too acidic or too alkaline, plants cannot absorb nutrients essential for healthy growth (see pages 45–49. **acid and alkaline soil (pH)**

Acidity and alkalinity are measured on a pH scale of 0 to 14 with 7.0 being the neutral point. Any figure above pH 7.0 is alkaline, and any figure below is acid. Most indoor plants prefer a slightly acid soil—a pH factor of 6.0 to 7.0. If the soil is too alkaline, a plant might show such symptoms as the discolored leaves that characterize iron or magnesium deficiencies (see page 48) or its roots will not develop properly with resultant retarded top growth. Many other factors of good plant growth are adversely affected by soil that is too alkaline.

Controls   Test soil with a home soil tester, a small kit that you can find in garden centers and plant stores. If soil is too acid (the pH will be low), add ground limestone to the soil. If soil is too alkaline (a high pH), add dusting sulfur to the soil. Follow package instructions carefully for accurate soil testing and for determining the proportions to use of necessary soil supplements. Acid fertilizers also help lower the pH. Peat and sphagnum moss added to soil are acid substances, but they act as buffers to absorb both excess acid and alkaline elements.

Plants affected   Plants preferring a more acid soil than most (a pH of 5.0 to 6.5) include: amaryllis, lilies, shrimp plant, azalea, bougainvillaea, camellia, century plant, gardenia, podocarpus, sea grape, holly, loquat, citrus, palms, asparagus fern.

animals versus plants Animals and plants do not always coexist happily indoors. Smashed pots, exposed roots, or top growth that has all but disappeared overnight might be explained by the activity of an adventurous pet. If a cat is not allowed to go outside, he chews on house plants, particularly anything that looks like grass, which is really what he wants, or has interesting berries or flowers.

Some cats sleep on the tops of large pots—which tends to compact the soil (see page 22)—and others use large pots as their litter boxes—which is of no help to delicate feeder roots and low-growing branches. Some enterprising cats knock pots off window sills if they find there's not enough room to sun themselves. And, worse, it appears that no two cats are interested in the same plant, or even a plant the cat has long ignored will one day become quite interesting to him.

Dogs, because they ordinarily go outdoors a lot, do not usually eat house plants and are not given to window-sill naps. However, curious puppies are a potential hazard to any plant within their reach. Many puppies will try to chew on plastic or rubber pots and saucers, and some puppies experiment with leaves and branches to see if they taste good. Grown-up dogs with long, heavy tails are obvious hazards to any plant located at tail-wagging height.

Birds, especially parrots and parakeets, present a threat to house plants if they are allowed out of their cages. They tug at and sometimes cut off whole branches quickly and indiscriminately, and nibble at leaves, flowers, and berries.

Controls   Provide window-sill room for cats, and avoid cultivating plants they seem to chew on consistently. If possible, give a cat a grassy-type plant of his own. Planting grass seed or catnip in a pot every month or so frequently proves an effective distraction. Mulching the tops of pots with large broken crocks discourages cats from lying or walking around on the soil. Avoid fine gravel unless you want your cat to mistake the pot for its litter box.

Put plants out of the reach of puppies or keep puppies out of the reach of plants until the puppies have outgrown the heavy chewing stage. There's not much you can do about enthusiastic tail-waggers except to set the plants up high. If window sills are low, raise plants on bricks or blocks of wood, or grow them in hanging pots.

If you let birds out of their cages, keep them out of rooms where plants are growing or chase them away from the growing area. Keep poinsettias, oleander, dieffenbachia, and stored bulbs well out of the reach of pets, because these plants and some bulbs are poisonous.

compacted soil   Water standing on top of the soil after you have watered the plant is the most obvious sign of compacted soil. Plants in such pots will show general deterioration, wilting, unnaturally slow growth, and too rapid loss of older leaves.

Compacted soil prevents water from percolating through the soil because air spaces between soil particles are compressed. Air cannot circulate around roots; soil does not hold sufficient moisture levels; and the drying-out process takes place too rapidly.

Controls   Compaction occurs most often in clay-based and fine-textured soils with little or no organic matter. Repot plant (see pages 34–36), adding peat moss, humus, perlite, or sand to the potting soil mixture.

Waterlogged soil is the most obvious indication of poor **drainage** drainage. Roots and top growth of most plants grown in constantly wet soil wilt and rot just as if the plant were overwatered (see pages 41–43). If you water a plant relatively infrequently and still the soil always feels wet and sodden, remove the plant from its pot and examine the drainage.

Drainage holes in clay flowerpots should be loosely covered with one or two curved pieces of broken clay pot to prevent soil from washing through along with excess water and clogging the holes. Plastic pots have several small holes or slits for drainage, but unlike clay pots, they are nonporous, so excess water that does not run out immediately after watering can evaporate only from the tops of pots. Plastic pots therefore require a layer one-half inch to an inch thick of crocking (small pieces of broken pot or pebbles) to prevent soil from washing through and to collect excess water until it evaporates or trickles out. Cover the crocking with nylon netting or an old stocking to prevent soil particles from sifting down and clogging the drainage area.

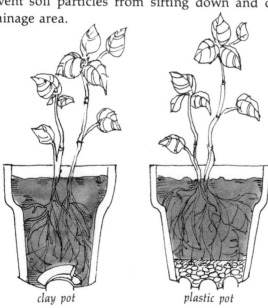

clay pot   *plastic pot*

Potting in containers without drainage holes almost guarantees drainage problems unless you are extremely careful not to overwater and unless you provide a drainage layer as in plastic pots.

Even with perfect crocking, a plant can suffer from poor drainage if the soil is poorly textured. Powdery soils tend to compact (see page 22); heavy, peaty soils soak up moisture and remain soaked longer than is good for many plants; and sandy soil drains very quickly, which is excellent for succulent plants but is too rapid for other plants.

Controls Insert crocking in plants purchased in uncrocked pots as soon as possible and according to the type of pot. If the root ball is already taking up so much room that there is no space left for crocking, repot the plant into the next larger-sized pot (see page 35). If plants have been suffering too long from poor drainage, roots may already be rotted away and top growth nearly gone. However, if at least part of the root system is still firm and white, cut off the rotting parts with a sharp knife and prune back corresponding dead or wilting top growth. Repot the plant into a pot just large enough to hold the root ball comfortably. To ensure ventilation, punch several quarter-inch holes in a plastic bag and enclose the plant in it for several weeks or until you see new top growth. Keep the plant out of strong light for a few days.

If poor drainage is caused by poorly textured soil, remove the plant from its pot and gently shake off as much soil as possible without grossly disturbing the roots. Follow the pruning and repotting procedures given above. If the plant requires fairly dry conditions, use a new soil mixture that is sandy or add sand or perlite to your potting soil. If the plant needs damp soil, add peat or humus to the potting soil, but add equal amounts of sand or perlite to ensure good drainage.

Plants affected See Watering (pages 41–43).

Browning leaf tips, yellowing leaf margins, stunted growth **humidity** or none at all, bud drop, shriveling, and wilting characterize too low humidity in the growing area. Excessive humidity is seldom a problem except in coastal areas during the summer or in terrariums, but if this is the case, plants will decay and rot and show darkening leaves and stems and the soft wilt that characterizes overwatering (see page 41). Plants in this condition are susceptible to bacterial and fungal invasions and pollution damage (see pages 32–33, 83–91).

During warm, rainy seasons indoor humidity might well equal outdoor humidity, but normally indoor humidity is much lower than plants are accustomed to outdoors. In cold weather, when indoor temperatures are high, humidity usually falls well below the lowest range tolerable for good plant growth. Fortunately, many indoor plants do adapt to low levels of humidity.

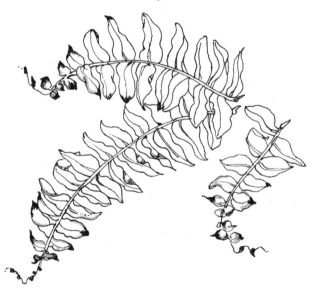

Controls A humidifier is the most effective method of controlling indoor humidity. A hygrometer, a small calibrating instrument that measures atmospheric moisture in the same fashion that a thermometer measures temperature, can be used to determine humidity levels, and the humidifier adjusted accordingly. If you have only a few plants, set them on a two- or three-inch layer of pebbles or gravel in water-filled trays to help raise the humidity in the growing area. Pots should sit above the water level which, as it evaporates, will help raise the humidity in the growing area. Cool room temperatures tend to raise humidity, and terrariums or any other glass-enclosed growing area provide ideal environments for plants requiring very high humidity. As bathrooms are frequently more humid than the rest of the home, you might consider growing ferns and other moisture-loving plants there.

Ventilate to reduce excess humidity. Open doors and windows; allow air to circulate without placing plants in direct drafts. Fans and air conditioners circulate air very well, but do not blow them directly on plants. Reduce watering to strengthen control of excess moisture.

Plants affected Too low humidity: ferns, carnivorous plants, caladium, anthurium, flame violet, oxalis, creeping fig, streptocarpus, some philodendrons, selaginella, ivies, sweet olive, maranta, iresine, and most flowering plants except cacti.

Too high humidity: This is not in itself necessarily a plant problem except that it promotes the development of leaf spot disease, molds and mildews (diseases), and the decay and rot characteristic of overwatering (see pages 41–43, 87, 88). All plants susceptible to these problems might be affected by conditions of prolonged excessive humidity. Roses, terrarium plants, and cacti and other succulents are the most vulnerable.

Insufficient light is the most common cause of weak, **light** stunted plant growth; distorted, discolored, or pale-toned leaves; massive defoliation; failure to produce fruit or flowers; and total collapse.

Too little light causes young plants to grow spindly and elongated with inadequate branching and misshapen or underdeveloped foliage. Older plants shed leaves, usually beginning from the bottom, cease growing, shrivel up, and finally die. Variegated plants revert to solid green, and leaves of all plants eventually turn yellow and drop off. Flowering and fruiting plants fail to produce buds, or if they do the buds shrivel up on the stems and fall off. In short, while some plants tolerate less light than others, no plant can live, much less grow, without receiving its minimum light level.

On the other hand, too much direct sun may cause the leaves to burn. They turn grayish where they are scorched and look bleached out elsewhere, and if the plant itself is one that cannot adjust to full direct sun, it will become limp, shrivel, and die. When a plant is growing in direct sun it needs more water (see page 42) and regular fertilization (see pages 45–49). Another problem of growing plants in direct sun, especially noonday and afternoon sun, is that they suffer from temperature that is too high (pages 39–40). When placing a plant in direct sun, help it to adjust by moving it into the sun by degrees, especially if it is unaccustomed to sunlight. Closing sheer curtains or closing blinds to half-mast will reduce this damaging intensity. (Follow the same precautions you will take when you start acquiring a summer tan.) The winter sun is much less intense than summer sun, so a plant that has been thriving all winter in sun all day may suddenly burn when exposed to summer sun. Morning sun, from sunrise to about 11:00 A.M., seldom causes a problem and is considered to be the most beneficial to plants both inside and out. It is considered bad practice to place house plants outside in direct sun for the summer.

Rx for Ailing House Plants

Light is measured by intensity and daylength. Intensity is classified as high, medium, and low. High light is ideally a southern exposure window, which, as it admits sun most of the day, provides the greatest intensity of light for the longest part of the day. Medium light can be eastern or western exposure windows, which admit morning or afternoon sun, respectively, and daylight for the remainder of the day. Low light is daylight with no direct sun, as found in northern exposure windows.

Certain variables can reduce light levels in any window. Trees, shrubbery, nearby buildings, screens, storm windows, curtains, blinds, and air pollution (see page 32) are all obstructing elements that reduce light intensity and daylengths. Keep in mind that light bounced off white walls is more intense than light absorbed by darker walls, that good reading light is equivalent to low plant light, and that plants set back even a foot or two or just to the side of a window receive considerably less light than plants centered directly in front of a window. The wall space between two windows is probably the darkest place in any room, unless the windows are catty-corner.

Daylength is the number of hours in each day that plants receive any degree of light. Short winter days produce a dormancy in many plants, but if the room temperature is below 50 degrees, they also promote flower-bud formation in other plants, especially Christmas cactus, chrysanthemums, and poinsettias. On the other hand, bromeliads and many annuals set buds only when daylengths are much longer (about twelve to sixteen hours). Some plants, particularly African violets, seem to bloom indiscriminately, no matter what the daylength is.

Controls   Either grow plants that adapt to your existing light conditions or adjust the light conditions to accommodate the plants. Before acquiring new plants, find out what their minimum light levels are. Most flowering and fruiting plants, cacti, and bromeliads require high light. Gesneriads, ficus, ferns, ivies, and palms are some species that thrive in medium light. Dracaenas, peperomia, philodendrons, aspidistra, and spathiphyllum adapt well to low light.

If the light levels in your home are insufficient, consider artificial lighting. Fluorescent, mercury-vapor, incandescent, or flood lamps can be used to supplement natural light or as a total light source in dark corners.

Unnaturally elongated growth indicates that plants are stretching toward the light. Put such plants at windowsill level or above and center in the window those needing the most light. Give pots a quarter-turn every few days to prevent lopsided growth.

Some young plants and many of the commonly grown foliage plants can adjust to relatively low light levels, although they may grow more slowly. Make such adjustments gradually by moving the plant every few days into less light until it reaches its destination. To compensate for the reduced light level or for weak winter light that all plants have to sustain, water less frequently and withhold fertilizer until there is definite evidence of new growth.

physical injuries   Physical injuries to plants are usually obvious, but they are often attributed to the wrong causes. Shipping damage accounts for many torn or broken leaves or branches on newly purchased plants. Even the most careful handling during packing and transporting cannot entirely prevent some physical damage.

If a pot was knocked over, you might not realize the extent of the damage right away, especially on large, very leafy or bushy plants. Besides bruised or torn leaves and branches, there may be root damage if the pot was smashed, and the plant will need some time to recover.

Rope or leather ties on hanging planters often rot away quite unnoticed, usually at the point where they are tied to the planter. Thus, you might come home someday and find a hanging plant in bits and pieces all over the floor and window sill.

Cacti and other succulents are usually potted in rather small pots to accommodate their shallow root systems. But if top growth becomes tall and heavy, the whole pot tends to topple over, and leaves and stems break off, or sometimes the top growth splits off altogether from the roots.

Drafts cause plants to sway toward one another with

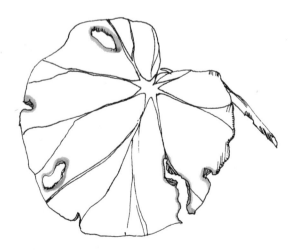

the result that leaves pressing against other leaves might cause weak or soft leaf tissue to split. Cactus needles can puncture or rip apart the leaves of closely adjacent plants, particularly broad-leaved evergreens. The smaller and more brittle leaves of succulent plants are sometimes knocked off by a watering can or your own hands.

Controls Remove torn or broken leaves and branches and discard them, unless they provide material for cuttings. Open wounds might decay and promote disease formation (see pages 34–36, 84–91). Avoid accidents by setting pots and saucers squarely on window sills, extending if possible the depth of some window sills to accommodate large plants.

If pots have been broken, repot plants that have been knocked down as quickly as possible to keep the root systems from drying out (see page 35). If immediate repotting is not convenient, at least enclose the root ball in a plastic bag.

Rope or leather ties of hanging planters should be reinforced with monofilament (nylon fishing line). The monofilament is nearly invisible and will not rot away from frequent waterings.

Top-heavy plants should be repotted in larger pots. If you think the root systems are too shallow for larger pots, rather than adding too much soil, fill in the difference with an extra-thick layer of drainage material (see page 23). The squat shapes of azalea pots (which come in all sizes) and bulb pans (which come in six- to nine-inch sizes) often serve as better anchors for heavy or bushy plants.

Prevent bruising or tearing of adjacent leaves by giving each plant a reasonable amount of space around it and by keeping plants out of direct drafts. Work delicately around succulent plants when watering or grooming in order to avoid knocking off brittle leaves. However, most leaves of succulent plants will root and form new little plants if they are simply laid on top of the soil or inserted very slightly into the soil.

pollution   If you live within seventy-five miles of an industrial center, some of your plants might react to high air-pollution levels with yellowing, spotted, or dropping leaves, distorted growth, burning leaf margins, general weakness, and finally death. Pollution can also stem from indoor factors, such as fireplace and cigarette smoke, manufactured gas, oil, kerosene, dust, and, of all things, ripening apples.

Smoke injury produces tip and marginal leaf burning (the edges and ends of leaves turn dry and brown), severe and rapid discoloration and defoliation, and sometimes sudden death wilt. As indoor smoke (which can also be produced by a faulty boiler) layers down from ceilings, tall plants might lose their tops while the bottom halves survive.

Smog, which is composed of unsaturated hydrocarbons and ozone, causes leaf spots, lesions, and dead areas on leaves that create openings for invasions by disease organisms (see pages 83–90). Some plants, such as ferns, decline within forty-eight hours if continuously exposed to smog. Soot, dust, and grease will coat leaves, causing weakness, discolorations, and slow decline. Kitchen plants are most likely to be affected.

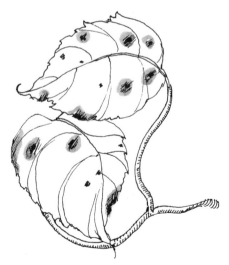

Manufactured gas, used for cooking and heating, causes browning, wilting, withering, or sudden death, because, even when burned, all the gas is not ignited. Natural gas, which is rarely harmful to plants, has replaced manufactured gas in most localities, and the use of any gas will probably have to replaced in the foreseeable future by other sources of energy.

Apples, as they ripen, give off ethylene gas, which may cause nearby foliage to bleach or turn yellow.

Controls High humidity and high temperatures intensify both outdoor and indoor pollution. Cross-ventilate, by opening doors and windows and/or using fans and air conditioners to reduce temperature and humidity levels, and to circulate air and help disperse smog, smoke, and other fumes. Ventilate rooms with fireplaces while the fire is lit, or remove plants from those rooms. During hot, damp weather, keep plants relatively dry and avoid allowing excess moisture to stand on the leaves.

Soot and dust can be cleaned off foliage with a spray mister or, for large-leaved plants, with a sponge. Wipe off grease with damp paper towels or damp sponges and soapy water, but use real soap or soap flakes, not detergent.

Tomato plants and Jerusalem cherry are the best indicators of gas leaks, because both plants respond quickly and dramatically with sudden death wilts. Jerusalem cherry turns black overnight. If gas leaks occur frequently and there's no apparent mechanical cause, notice whether drafts are blowing out pilot lights.

Ripening apples should be kept in the refrigerator or, if left out in bowls or baskets, out of rooms where plants are growing.

Rx for Ailing House Plants

repotting and potting-on   Repotting and potting-on, recommended as a cure for a variety of plant ailments, can themselves become plant problems if certain procedures are not properly followed.

Repotting is the process of taking the plant out of its pot, changing the soil or drainage or possibly root-pruning and then putting the plant back in the same pot or the same-sized pot or a smaller pot. Repotting is indicated when plants suffer from compacted soil, poor drainage, salt damage, soil-borne insects, or inadequate nutrition.

When it is necessary to prune roots remove all of the soil using a gentle flow of lukewarm water. Be gentle but don't be timid. After the soil is removed, cut off all damaged, mushy, broken, infected or overly long roots. Be sure

to use sharp scissors or pruning shears. When removing roots cut at the joints or back at the point where the root originates. Do not let the healthy roots dry out.

To repot, spread the roots and gently work a good potting soil between them. Water the plant and place in a plastic bag punched with several half-inch holes for air circulation. Keep the covering on for about one week.

Potting-on is the process of moving the plant into the next larger-sized pot; it is indicated when plants repeatedly wilt within hours after watering, bottom leaves turn yellow and drop off, or new growth is dwarfed or stunted. If any or all of these conditions prevail, turn the plant out of its pot, taking care to hold the root ball intact. If the roots are twined around the outside of the root ball in a fairly dense mass, the plant is pot-bound, that is, it has outgrown that pot. Once the root system outgrows the pot, there is not enough soil area left to hold water long enough for plants to absorb it. The plants thus affected react to insufficient water by putting all their growing energies into new growth with consequent loss of older growth or by producing stunted new growth to conserve a limited water supply. If the pot-bound condition persists too long, the plant simply wilts no matter how much water it receives, and repeated wilting eventually weakens the entire structure of the plant.

Controls   Ordinarily, when you take a plant out of its pot, you should hold the root ball together as intactly as possible. However, if you are washing off soil-borne insects or pruning away rotted roots, it might be necessary to remove all soil from the roots. Take care not to pull or tear at large roots or break off small feeder roots. Gently shake most of the soil off the root system and wash the rest off under a slow lukewarm faucet. Use a small sharp kitchen knife for root-pruning. After repotting, give the plant high humidity by misting (page 95) several times daily or enclosing it loosely in a plastic bag with several small holes punched in it for several weeks until the root system has regenerated.

Repot plants maintaining the same soil line on the main stem or trunk as in the original pot. If the old soil line is set below the soil surface, roots will deteriorate and top growth decline. If the soil line is set higher than the soil surface, top roots are exposed and will die, and the plant might topple over. You can distinguish the soil line by the color of the plant's trunk or crown, which is lighter above the soil line and darker below.

Whatever the reason for potting-on or repotting, the pot should be no larger or no smaller than necessary to hold the root system comfortably within a thin layer of soil around the sides and bottom of the pot. Soil in pots that are too large becomes waterlogged, and plants suffer from overwatering and/or poor drainage. If roots are pruned and it is necessary to repot into a smaller pot, be sure it is not so small that you are jamming the roots in and thus bruising them or breaking them off.

Avoid letting roots dry out while repotting. If, for some reason, you must interrupt your work, moisten the root ball and enclose it in a plastic bag. Exposed root systems must be kept damp at all times. If you dig up garden annuals for potting indoors, scoop up the roots gently with a generous amount of soil, moisten, and enclose them in a plastic bag or set them in a pail of water until you are ready to pot them. Root balls of mail-order plants that have been shipped unpotted or of any plants being transferred from one pot to another should be treated the same way.

A crusty white substance coating the top of the soil or the **salt** rims of pots indicates an excess of salt build-up in the soil. **damage** Affected plants show tip and marginal leaf burn, root burning and deterioration, and thick, dwarfed leaves with sunken breathing pores on leaf undersides. All these conditions reduce water evaporation and air circulation.

Old soil, repeated fertilizing, and giving plants too little water at one time can contribute to heavy salt accumulations. In some localities, salt concentrations in tap water are too high for good plant growth.

Water, as it runs out of drainage holes, tends to leach out some of the salt accumulation, but in containers with no drainage holes the leaching-out process is considerably hampered.

Controls   If tap water is too saline, mix it with rain, melted snow, or distilled water. Flush out excess salts by watering heavily and repeatedly until water pours out of drainage holes (you will be literally flooding the plant).

If pot rims are heavily encrusted, it's probably time to repot the plant. Clay pots absorb much of the excess salt; if salt build-up occurs rather frequently and/or your tap water is saline, use clay pots. Use a slightly acid soil (see page 19).

Most indoor plants thrive in a room temperature range of **temperature** 55 to 85 degrees Fahrenheit. However, drafty windows, corners, and floors of cool rooms may be as much as 20 degrees colder than the rest of the room. Plants touching window panes in winter can freeze if the outdoor temperature drops below freezing. Leaves of plants grown in a colder temperature range than they like will curl up, turn brown, and drop off.

Leaves, especially the older ones, that turn yellow, wilt, and drop off reflect a higher room temperature range than the plant can adapt to. Some plants might die within a few days if constantly exposed to too high temperatures; others might survive longer but become very susceptible to the development of several types of insects (see pages 55, 69). Plants sitting on top of or near radiators or on the floor over the boiler in the cellar are growing in tempera-

too cold

too hot

tures that are much warmer than the rest of the room. If too high temperatures produce wilting in a plant whose soil is kept constantly damp, roots will start rotting away.

Most plants, whatever temperature range they thrive in, will grow better if the nighttime temperature is 10 degrees less than the daytime temperature. Plants, such as dieffenbachia, philodendrons, maranta, caladium, aglaonema, and some bromeliads, that originate in low elevations near the equator where temperatures are constantly warm can be grown indoors in warm rooms without a nighttime drop. Other plants such as podocarpus, pittosporum, auracaria, acuba, ivies, and bamboo are tropicals that grow at high altitudes, thus making them good choices for cool windows or sun porches and air-conditioned rooms. Knowing a plant's native climate will help you determine its optimal temperature range.

Controls   Read temperatures at different times of the day and night in projected or existing growing areas and in problem areas. Use weather stripping for drafty windows, and place sheets of newspaper between plants and windowpanes on frosty nights.

Plants that droop in west or south windows might be reacting to hot afternoon sun. Move these plants a foot or two away from the window, particularly in summer, or partially shade them with sheer curtains or Venetian blinds drawn at half-mast.

If you must use the top of a radiator as a plant shelf, set the plants in trays of gravel and water and, in the winter, cover the radiator top with an asbestos sheet.

If you have steam pipes and radiator heat, turn the radiators off as much of the time as possible in the winter and particularly at night. If possible, lower thermostats at night in rooms where plants are grown, and move cool-temperature plants from other rooms into these. Cool-temperature plants do well in air conditioning, but keep them out of the line of drafts.

Corky scabs or protrusions on the undersides of leaves or **watering** on branches; rotting roots; decaying and dropping foliage; blackening and wilting stems and leaves; and soft, mushy-textured succulent leaves are all symptoms of overwatering. The same symptoms might appear to indicate fungus diseases but actually precede a fungus invasion, which usually follows the advanced stages of overwatering damage.

If plants gradually wilt and soil is very dry and shrinks inward from the sides of pots, the problem is underwatering. Other symptoms of underwatering: foliage of broad-leaved plants darkens and turns crisp; older leaves drop; and leaves and stems of succulent plants tend to turn pale and shrivel up.

The watering process itself forces carbon dioxide out of the root zone and pulls oxygen into it. Most plants will suffer serious root damage and eventually die if they are kept continuously wet or dry.

The frequency with which to water any plant depends on the plant's native growing conditions. Plants originating in dry areas should be watered very thoroughly but allowed to dry out for several days before rewatering. Poke your finger an inch or two into the soil of large pots to make sure the soil is really dry. However, bear in mind that no plant can survive remaining dry indefinitely. Even desert cacti are accustomed to heavy rainfalls, flash floods, and winter snow in their native environment.

Plants requiring constant moisture should also be thoroughly soaked but re-watered when the soil feels just towel-damp. Most indoor plants fall into a middle range; their soil should be watered as soon as it has dried out.

It is impossible to put any plant on a regular year-round watering schedule. Most require more frequent watering in spring and summer when high temperatures promote rapid evaporation and when rapidly growing root systems absorb water quickly. Plants growing in cool temperatures and high humidity dry out slowly, and plants in a dormant state need less frequent watering than usual. Clay pots permit evaporation from their sides as well as from the top because they are porous; so plants in clay pots dry out more quickly than those in plastic pots.

Controls Since some of the symptoms of overwatering—such as wilting and darkening leaves—resemble those of underwatering, you should use your judgment. If the soil is always or nearly always damp or wet and the plant appears to be rotting away, it's probably been overwatered. Cultivate the surface soil (stir it up gently with a fork) to encourage aeration, and put the plant in a warmer, well-ventilated location until it dries out, but do not put it in a draft. Cut off injured or decayed vegetation. If these measures do not speed recovery, the plant is beyond salvation. If there is any uninjured plant material, you might want to use it for cuttings; otherwise, discard the plant altogether.

Underwatering is quickly obvious because the plant wilts with a dry look rather than a rotting look, and the soil is very dry most of the time. The cause of the problem may not be the frequency with which you water but the amount of water you use. If you give a plant too little water at a time so that all the soil is not saturated, the bottom roots receive little or no water, and the plant exhibits the same symptoms as if it had been watered too infrequently. To ensure thorough soaking, water slowly and evenly over the entire soil surface until excess water runs out of drainage holes, but do not allow pots to sit in water-filled jardinieres or saucers. A long-spouted watering can is the best device for watering potted plants, because you can poke the long spout in between or under the leaves of dense or bushy plants, thus permitting even watering of the soil and preventing excessive soaking of the foliage. Also, the leaves of some plants tend to rot if water is repeatedly poured on them.

Before rewatering, allow the plant to dry out enough to meet its normal requirements for water. Remove damaged foliage and stems. Underwatered plants usually perk up soon after a thorough watering, and you can speed up recovery by enclosing the plant loosely in a plastic bag for a few hours after watering.

Plants affected   Overwatering: cacti and other succulents; begonias, peperomia, pileas, and other plants with semi-succulent brittle, fleshy-textured leaves and stems; bulb plants, such as freesias, amaryllis, and narcissus; dracaenas; geraniums; and most gesneriads.

Underwatering: ferns, cissus, ficus, ivies, philodendron, bog and carnivorous plants, flowering plants except cacti, ligustrum, and all seedlings.

Chapter 3

Nutritional Deficiencies

All plants require sixteen essential chemical elements for survival and healthy growth: carbon, hydrogen, oxygen, nitrogen, phosphorus, potassium, calcium, magnesium, iron, and seven trace elements. The first three are present in air and water; the remainder in soil and fertilizer. Nitrogen, phosphorus, and potassium are the major components of any fertilizer, but calcium, magnesium, and iron should also be present in substantial amounts. Plants require very tiny amounts of the trace elements: manganese, boron, copper, zinc, molybdenum, sulfur, and chlorine.

Inorganic fertilizers, composed of chemical compounds, are usually less expensive than organic fertilizers, which are derived from animal or vegetable wastes. Organic fertilizers are also less likely to supply all essential nutrients. In the horticultural trade, a "complete fertilizer" refers to one that contains nitrogen, phosphorus, and potassium with an uncertain number of other elements if any; a literally complete fertilizer, one that includes all elements, is referred to as a "well-balanced fertilizer." Read container labels; if a so-called complete fertilizer lacks certain elements, you must supplement it with a well-balanced fertilizer. The numbers, such as 5-10-5, printed on fertilizer labels just below the brand name, refer to the percentages of nitrogen, phosphorus, and potassium (the N,P,K) in that fertilizer. Other elements are given in an ingredients list. If plants lack some elements, they respond with such symptoms of ill health as leaf discolor, stunted growth, distorted shapes, or general weakening. All nutritional difficulties, however, are eliminated if plants are potted in organically rich soil and fertilized regularly with a well-balanced fertilizer. Regardless of what the composition of the soil is, fertilizing should begin as soon as the plant is potted or as soon as you acquire it.

Fertilizers, such as bone meal or Osmacote, that decompose slowly with successive waterings and release their nutrients over a period of time need be applied only every five or six months, depending on the type or brand. Apply other fertilizers about every two weeks during the spring and summer active growing season, about once a month during the fall and winter periods of slow growth, and not at all when plants are dormant.

In computing dosages, always cut the recommended amounts on container labels by one-third to one-half. Even at the height of the active growing season, conditions indoors are such that they will not encourage the run-away, rampant growth you might find outdoors; so fertilizing should be scaled down accordingly to meet the slower and more controlled indoor growth. Err on the side of too little rather than too much. Too strong and/or too frequent fertilizing burns plant roots and consequently kills top growth.

nitrogen (N) Nitrogen is the part of the chlorophyll molecule that gives healthy plants their green color. A nitrogen deficiency results in a stunted plant with yellowish leaves—a condition called chlorosis. Older leaves fade first; if the deficiency is severe, they will turn brown and die. Excess nitrogen causes an overlong growing period that retards maturity and produces a weak, fleshy plant. In this condition, the plant is susceptible to insects and diseases; roots burn, and top growth repeatedly wilts as if the plant were not getting enough water.

Controls Bone meal, dried blood, animal manure, and fish emulsion are all the best commercial sources of nitrogen. A complete inorganic fertilizer supplies sufficient quantities of nitrogen. Use small concentrations fairly frequently.

phosphorus (P) Phosphorus strengthens roots and stems and promotes seed formation and flower color. A deficiency retards growth and intensifies green leaf color until the foliage turns purple or bronze or becomes mottled in light and dark tones. Older leaves are more subject to discoloration.

Controls Complete fertilizers include this element, but bone meal is an especially good source.

potassium (K) Potassium is important because it strengthens disease resistance, but it also promotes abundant flowering and stem development. A deficiency shows as tip and marginal burn first on lower leaves and later advancing up the plant. Leaves crinkle and turn inward, and the plant stops growing.

Controls Light, regular applications of a complete fertilizer provide plants with enough potassium. Wood ashes are an excellent source.

calcium (Ca) Calcium aids flower development and stem and root growth. A deficiency occurs if soil is excessively acidic (see page 19), with the result that terminal leaf buds fail to develop fully and new leaves are incompletely formed or have irregular marginal shapes.

Controls   Limestone is a commonly used concentrated source of calcium, but it raises the alkalinity of the soil (see page 19). Sources of calcium that do not change the pH factor of soil are wood ashes, chicken grit, oyster shells, or crushed eggshells. Well-balanced fertilizers include sufficient amounts of calcium. Test soil with a soil tester to determine the pH factor, and correct for alkalinity if soil proves to be too acidic.

magnesium (Mg)   The central constituent of the chlorophyll molecule, magnesium is essential for chlorophyll synthesis. A deficiency produces chlorosis or yellowing of older leaf tissue, as does a nitrogen deficiency, but in a magnesium deficiency the leaf veins remain green. Occasionally leaves turn white at the margins or develop a purplish cast that gradually turns brown.

Controls   Soil that is too alkaline inhibits the plant's ability to absorb magnesium. Test for the pH factor in the soil with a soil tester (see page 19), and correct for acidity if this is the case. Watering the plant with one tablespoon of Epsom salts to a quart of water corrects magnesium deficiency, but use a well-balanced fertilizer regularly to prevent recurrence.

iron   Like magnesium deficiencies, iron deficiencies also occur in soil that is too alkaline with the result that leaf tissue turns yellow while veins remain green (see page 19). Iron is not part of the chlorophyll molecule but is essential to chlorophyll synthesis. A deficiency further shows up as stunted growth and unnaturally curled leaves.

Controls Correct soil for acidity and use a chelated iron sold in plant stores to restore iron to the plant.

Seven more elements are essential to plant growth but they **trace** must be present only in minuscule quantities. Larger **elements** amounts of any one are toxic to plants.

A lack of manganese causes young leaves to turn yellow while all veins, even the tiny ones, remain green, giving the leaves a network appearance.

A boron deficiency causes new leaves to stop growing and start withering from the base of the leaf. Leaves turn downward, and eventually the entire leaf bud dies.

If copper is not present, leaves are either extra large and unnaturally dark green or very small and quickly shed. Growing tips die back exuding a reddish-brown gummy discharge.

Zinc deficiencies produce small, crinkled, chloritic new leaves with such short internodes between leaves that the appearance is one of untypical rosettes. If the condition remains uncorrected, general defoliation begins from the base of the plant and proceeds upward.

The absence of molybdenum causes mottled, curling leaves and irregular marginal shapes.

Sulfur deficiencies resemble nitrogen deficiencies (see page 46–47) but to a less severe degree. General growth and fruiting are retarded. As sulfur is used to acidify soil (see page 19), its shortage might also generate iron and magnesium deficiencies.

Chlorine is required for plant growth in tiny amounts, but most indoor plants receive far too much from chlorinated water used in most cities. A moderate excess causes leaf tissue to thicken and become brittle. A great excess burns and destroys plant roots. Chlorine evaporates or is neutralized by sunlight if water is allowed to stand for a day in a sunny spot before being used to water plants.

Chapter 4

Insect
Pests

In an outdoor garden some insects are beneficial and necessary, and others are definitely harmful, but in any indoor growing situation it is safe to assume that any insect or any sign of an insect means danger for the plant so affected. Unchecked, insect invasions on indoor plants will spread around to other plants and possibly result in the death of all your plants.

Insects appear from a variety of sources. Many are brought in from outside on your hands, gardening tools, or clothing, by animals that brush against plants, or even by a strong breeze blowing through an open window. Some of the larger insects are summer pests that find their way into heated houses in the fall where they hibernate for the winter and look for food among indoor plants. Others, especially the very tiny and most common indoor plant pests, may develop from microscopic eggs that lodged on the plant even before you brought it home.

Obviously it is impractical to examine every crack and crevice in your home every day to make sure insects have not found their way indoors. And it is equally impractical to go over plants every day with a magnifying glass to detect insect eggs. But a close look at plants from time to time, perhaps when you water them, should reveal the early signs of insect invasions. If you isolate and treat the afflicted plant immediately, you will not only rescue it but you will prevent the invasion from spreading to other plants.

ants   Ants are not usually a major indoor plant pest, but several small garden and household species are drawn to plants covered with the sticky, sweet honeydew secreted by mealy bugs, aphids, and scale. Ants then add to the injury already done. Ants also make the problem of eradicating their host insects more difficult, because they move around very fast and tend to carry their hosts from one plant to another.

Whole colonies of ants might, under certain circumstances, live and work together in planter boxes or flowerpots, where they dig up and cart away seedlings or newly planted seeds. The roots of the remaining plants are seriously disturbed by the ants' burrowing activities. Some ants spread bacterial and fungal organisms that further damage plants.

Controls   Keep the growing area and potting benches clean and free of the debris and decaying vegetation in which ants tend to colonize. Treat soil surfaces, potting benches, growing areas, and individual ant hills with a soil drench, such as V-C-13, or Malathion used as a drench. If ants are attracted by other insects, you must then, of course, treat plants accordingly for those insects.

Plants affected   Seedlings, newly planted seeds, and plants commonly host to aphids, mealy bugs, and scale.

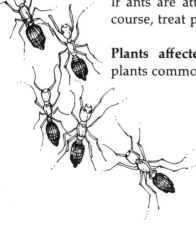

Aphids are tiny (but quite visible) soft-bodied, round in- **aphids**
sects that are among the most common indoor plant pests
but are also among the most easily eradicated. They tend
to congregate in masses around growing tips, where plant
tissue is most tender.

Aphids damage plants by sucking plant juices, causing deformed, curled new leaves, buds, and flowers. Some
are carriers of disease (see pages 84–89). They are most
easily detected by the sticky honeydew substance they secrete which also attracts ants and eventually coats leaf
surfaces with a sooty, black mold. Some aphids fly and
some crawl, but most are likely to be distributed by hand
or brought indoors on tools or pots, or carried around by
ants.

Some species naturally feed on just one plant; others
tend to migrate from plant to plant. Certain species in the
newly hatched stage feed on new growth, where their
feeding releases a toxin that causes galls (bumps or protu-
berances) to form on branches. Each gall contains a colony
of young aphids that live and feed within until maturity,

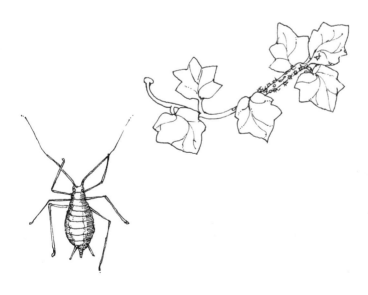

when the galls open and release the adults for feeding and breeding activity on other plants.

Controls   A mild infestation may be checked with a forceful spray of lukewarm water either plain or mixed with soap flakes. For stronger control, add a teaspoon of nicotine sulfate to a gallon of soapy water. Rotenone- or pyrethrum-based sprays formulated for indoor plants are effective, but for a serious infestation Malathion is the best control.

Cut off and burn stems with galls, and discard badly infested plants. Uninfested stems and branches may be used for cuttings after spraying with Malathion.

Plants affected   Avocado, citrus, cyclamen, begonias, chrysanthemums, dieffenbachia, gardenia, geranium, fats-hedera, sea grape, palms, summer annuals potted up for winter bloom, and, in general, plants grown in cool temperatures. Ferns are sometimes affected, but spraying with most chemicals kills the ferns, so you may use only non-chemical controls or a systemic insecticide applied to the soil.

Gall-producing aphids attack gardenias, gesneriads, asparagus ferns, begonias, fuchsia, poinsettia, and ficus.

The large yellow-and-black narcissus bulb fly that resembles a small bumblebee lays its eggs at the base of leaves or in the necks of various Dutch bulbs. The eggs hatch into fat white maggots that bore into bulbs and feed on them, thus causing exterior brown scars and eventually a soft, mushy texture. Affected bulbs do not grow or at best they produce stunted, yellow foliage and no flowers. The flies are not native to this country but their larvae frequently appear in imported bulb shipments. **bulb pests**

Bulb mites are tiny, spotted white-and-brown insects that lay eggs behind bud scales. The young nymphs feed in great masses on each bulb and cause the bulbs to become soft and mushy and the foliage, if any, to grow stunted or yellowed with distorted bloom or none at all. The adult flies that are drawn to bulbs in the first place by decaying plant material can themselves spread bacterial and fungal infections to healthy bulbs.

The bulb scale mite, which is related to and resembles the cyclamen mite, feeds between leaves and flowers at the neck of the bulb. As a result, the bulb becomes soft and spongy, with scarred streaks and injured flower and leaf tissue.

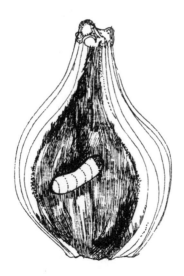

The tulip bulb aphid is a powdery insect about one-tenth inch long that comes in various bright colors and infests bulbs below the soil level. It also feeds on stored bulbs. Top growth becomes stunted and distorted, and finally dies.

Controls Examine bulbs carefully for soft spots and rough scars before you purchase them or when you receive a mail-order shipment. Good bulbs of any variety should be firm, white, unmarked, and well covered with a thin, papery outer skin, usually brown.

If you receive infested bulbs, discard and burn the obviously badly infested ones. Cut out soft spots and swollen areas on lightly infested bulbs, and treat with a bulb dust, such as Gladiolus and Bulb Dust or Bulb Saver.

If you do not plant right away, store bulbs in a cool, dry place; the bottom of a refrigerator will do for apartment dwellers. Bulbs may be treated with bulb dusts before planting or storing.

Spray systemic insecticides, such as Systemic, on foliage, or use as a dip for infested bulbs.

Plants affected Narcissus, amaryllis, hyacinth, scilla, crocus, tulip, freesia.

Caterpillars include those fuzzy little "hedgehog" crea- **caterpillars**
tures that roll up into a ball if touched. Both the fuzzy **and cutworms**
species and unfuzzy larger cutworms, all mutlicolored,
spotted, or striped, are juvenile forms of moths and but-
terflies. Many hide in the soil and around pots by day and
emerge at night to chew on leaves, buds, and flowers; it
is not uncommon for an entire plant to be stripped overnight. Some cutworms topple young plants at the soil line
or slash through whole branches or flower heads of larger
plants. Other insects can similarly devastate plants, but
caterpillars can often be pinpointed by the dark specks of
excrement that they leave on remaining foliage.

One species, the greenhouse leaf tier, may be identified by the evidence of light webs and chewed-away un-
dersurfaces of leaves. The light-green caterpillar larvae of
this insect feed underneath leaves, then roll them over and
secure themselves inside with silken webs.

Caterpillars and cutworms are not ordinarily attracted
to indoor conditions, but are frequently brought in on cut
flowers or garden tools.

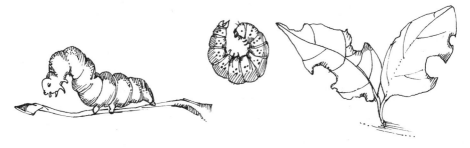

Controls Hand-pick and destroy them, especially if you
just see a few. If you suspect that there's more than meets
the eye, water plants with a soil drench, such as V-C-13
or a Malathion solution. Spray under and around pots and
foliage with Malathion.

Plants affected Primarily fleshy-textured and soft-tissued
plants.

cockroaches   Cockroaches are brown beetlelike insects that invade heated households in cool wet weather and hide under and behind furniture, around baseboards, in TV sets and radios, and in damp, tight places, such as drainpipes, cracks around plumbing fixtures, and between plant pots and saucers. Indoors, roaches feed on garbage, exposed food, and, not infrequently, house plants. Plants affected present a thoroughly chewed-up appearance.

Controls   Ant and roach sprays can be used around potting benches and in the growing area but should not be sprayed on foliage. Malathion is a good control for roaches and can be sprayed anywhere except in food areas. Roaches seem to keep evolving into stronger and more resistant generations. If the infestation is really heavy, consult local pest-control authorities to find out what the current effective control is in your locality.

    If you see just a few roaches, hit them with a fly swatter. Pine-oil-based household cleaners sprayed full strength around the growing area or in other places where roaches tend to congregate will discourage future roach invasions and slowly kill existing roaches. Be careful not to let the spray come in contact with the foliage.

Plants affected   Most fleshy-textured or soft-tissued plants and new growth. Because roaches are attracted to dampness, plants that are ordinarily kept damp and humid most of the time, especially terrarium plants, are particularly susceptible. Decaying vegetation encourages roach feeding, so growing areas should be kept clean and free of wilted and dead growth.

Crickets sound beautiful at night in an August garden, but **crickets** if they find their way into the house they hide by day under pots and saucers, around baseboards and in trash, soil, and decaying vegetation, and feed at night on new plant growth. If new leaves seem to disappear only at night, suspect crickets. They are fairly large black or brown insects that are related to grasshoppers, which they somewhat resemble. Terrariums seem especially susceptible, particularly if the terrarium harbors decaying plants.

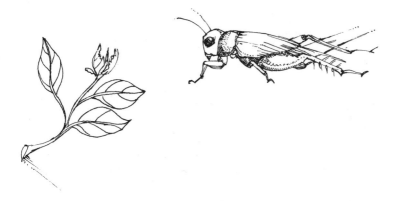

Controls Hand-picking will do for a few crickets, as they are easily spotted. Poison baits are effective controls for a severe invasion. If there are many crickets, it is possible that eggs have been laid in the soil. Drench the soil with V-C-13, a nicotine sulfate solution, Malathion, or a systemic insecticide.

Plants affected Seedlings, new growth, any fruits or vegetables, grassy or soft-tissued plants.

earthworms   Earthworms are pink, brown, or green segmented, elongated creatures that live in the soil and surface only at night or by day just after watering or if soil is kept moist. They are two to ten inches long and are capable of great expansion or contraction. Though essential for fertilization and soil aeration in gardens and fields, in pots they dig too many tunnels for the small space, thus causing the drying out of root balls, soil upheaval, and consequent general damage to roots.

Controls   You can hand-pick and destroy them or put them outside if you have a garden. Carefully examine the root balls of plants that have summered outdoors and annuals to be potted for indoor growing, and pick out earthworms before bringing plants inside. Sterilize garden soil before potting, or use presterilized soil for all indoor plants, because unsterilized soil is likely to harbor earthworms.

Plants affected   Plants potted in unsterilized soil, moisture-loving plants.

These dark-brown, beetlelike insects, identified easily by **earwigs** a distinct forceps-like attachment at the ends of their bodies, are found mostly in the coastal states. Though not commonly drawn to indoor living, they feed on the foliage of many flowering plants and hide in clothes drying outside and around dead or decaying foliage. Thus they are carried into the house with the laundry or cut flowers. Once inside, they crawl rapidly and hide by day in sofa cushions, under dishes, or in clothing. At night they emerge to look for food, frequently among indoor plants. The young chew green shoots; the adults eat holes in leaves, flowers, and fruit.

Controls Hand-pick earwigs off pots and foliage and destroy them. Apply poison baits or dusts around house foundations, fences, and other hiding places to help catch these pests before they come into the house. Spray plants with Malathion or spray with an aerosol roach spray around the growing area without hitting the foliage.

Plants affected New, tender growth and herbaceous (soft-tissued) plants.

fungus gnats (mushroom flies) These are tiny, sooty, grayish black flies that seldom feed on plants, but you might see them swarming over foliage because they are attracted to light. Eggs laid in the soil hatch into threadlike white maggots that burrow through the soil, or embed themselves in root tissue, and eat small feeding roots and root hairs and crowns of plants. Afflicted plants suffer from root rot, with consequent slow, weak top growth and yellowing leaves. Root feeding also produces wounds that can permit entry of disease organisms (see pages 90–91).

Controls Sterilize potting soil or use presterilized commercial soil mixes, and keep growing conditions on the dry side. V-C-13, a nicotine sulfate solution, or Malathion poured through soil kills eggs and maggots. Adult flies can be eradicated by a general-purpose house-plant aerosol insecticide.

Plants affected As the gnats tend to breed in decaying vegetation, any plant potted in moist, humusy soil might be affected.

These are the larvae of a variety of flies, moths, sawflies, **leaf** and beetles that eat leaf tissue between the upper and **miners** lower leaf surfaces and cause slender, winding trails, tunnels, and blisters throughout the leaf. Some larvae roll the tips of leaves over, get inside, and feed until it is time to spin cocoons, which they fasten to the leaves rolled in from the margins. The chrysanthemum-leaf miner larva causes leaves to dry up and hang on plants, and fills its tunnels with black specks of excrement.

Controls Remove and destroy infested, damaged and rolled leaves, and isolate afflicted plants from their neighbors until you're certain there are no repeated infestations. Keep growing conditions fairly dry. If the infestation is advanced, spray repeatedly with systemic insecticides, such as Isotox or Systemic, or apply systemic granules, sold under the same trade names, to the soil.

Plants affected Azalea, browallia, African violets and other gesneriads.

leaf rollers These caterpillars, the larvae of various moths, feed on leaves that they roll around themselves for protection. The oblique-banded and carnivorous species are the ones most likely to infest indoor plants. The former is the all-too-familiar pale-green, black-headed rose leaf tier that first mines open leaves, then works inside rolled areas. It can sometimes be detected early by eggs laid by the adult moth in overlapping masses on branches of ornamental shrubs or rose leaves. The omnivorous leaf roller is yellow-brown and feeds in much the same manner as the rose leaf tier.

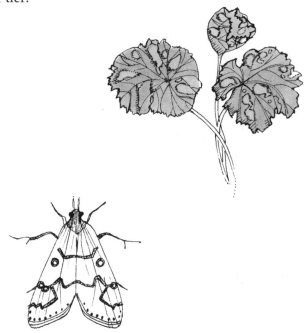

Controls Pick off and destroy rolled leaves. Contact insecticides, such as Malathion or Isotox can be sprayed on foliage.

Plants affected Roses, geraniums, oleander, begonias, carnations, annuals.

The mealy bug is actually a scale insect, but instead of **mealy** having a small hard shell, it is covered with layers of a **bugs** white waxy substance. Lodged on plants, mealy bugs appear at a glance to be little bits of cotton batting tucked into leaf axes or resting along stems and branches. Mealy bugs suck sap from plant tissues and the result is stunted growth, wilting, and general defoliation. Eventually the plant collapses altogether and dies. These pests also secrete a honeydew substance that attracts ants (see page 52) and forms a growing medium for fungi.

Some species attack as many as twenty different plants or plant families. Unlike most other species, the ground mealy bug, a European import, lives on terminal roots, especially those of cacti. All species are persistent and particularly difficult to eradicate.

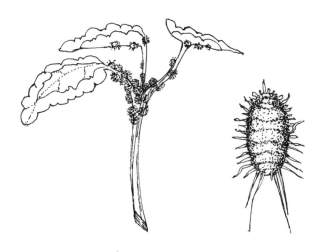

Controls The time-honored remedy of dabbing each mealy bug with a Q-tip dipped in alcohol or nail-polish remover is a waste of time. For one thing, it's boring to sit for hours picking hundreds of bugs off one plant, and for another, alcohol or acetone damages foliage. Also, should you miss so much as one female mealy bug, she alone can lay as many as six hundred new eggs, so all your efforts will be as good as useless. Strong measures are called for, as the mealy bug is among the five or six insect pests most commonly found on indoor plants and most damaging, as well as being extremely persistent. Systemic pesticides, such as Isotox or Systemic, sprayed at weekly intervals for three weeks should effectively eradicate both the pest insects themselves and any residue of eggs.

Ferns cannot be sprayed, but systemic granules applied to the soil will eventually rid ferns of mealy bugs. However, here you will have to pick off the first batch to prevent them from further damaging the plant before the systemic has a chance to work its way into plant tissue. If the picking process seems too tedious or you are dealing with very large ferns or a great many of them, spray them with a nicotine sulfate solution, but use the systemic granules as well.

Plants affected   Palms, cacti and other succulents, coleus, ferns, gardenia, dracaenas, dieffenbachia, cissus, citrus, ivies, avocado, crassula, lantana, oleander, schefflera, African violets and other gesneriads, ficus, aglaonema, hibiscus, dizygotheca, hoya, pittosporum, podocarpus, herbs.

Millipedes are multilegged, many-segmented hard-shelled **millipedes** worms that are fast, active crawlers. Indoors they coil up **and** in rich organic soil, where they feed on roots, tubers, **centipedes** bulbs, seeds, and fleshy stems. In strong light, they hide under pots and saucers. Chewed parts of seedlings and young stem growth are a common indication of these pests, but you might see the insects before the damage is extensive.

Centipedes dwell mainly under the surface of the soil, where they prune root systems to the stage where the top growth becomes completely stunted before it finally dies. The true centipede, a rather large, conspicuous creature common to the Rocky Mountains, is not a garden pest; what we are concerned with here is a symphylan, commonly called a centipede because it looks like one. The young symphylans are tiny white worms that hatch from eggs laid in the soil. Like the adults, each has twelve pairs of legs that carry them around rather quickly through the root zone, where they feed on root hairs, new root growth, and underground parts of stems.

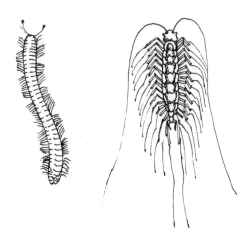

Controls You can find millipedes easily if you look for them in dim light; destroy them. For symphylans, you should repot the plant in sterilized soil after first pruning off damaged roots and washing all the old soil off the plants (see pages 34–35). Insects can be sprayed with contact insecticides, such as Malathion or any house-plant aerosol spray. For symphylans, drench the soil with V-C-13 or a Malathion solution.

Keep growing areas clean, and potting benches clean, because decaying vegetation attracts these pests.

Plants affected As these insects are drawn to rich, humusy soil, any ornamental or flowering plant grown in soil containing large proportions of peat moss or humus may prove attractive (and edible) to them. Camellias, philodendrons, and other aroids are particularly susceptible.

Mites are so indigenous to the indoor garden that the **mites**
frequency of mite infestations is probably as great as all
other insect infestations put together. Commonly called
red spider or spider mite, the mite is not a true insect but,
rather, belongs to the class Arachnida, which also includes
spiders, scorpions, dog ticks, and chiggers. Most species
proliferate rapidly and furiously in the hot, dry growing
environments found in most homes, but cool temperatures
and high humidity encourage the breeding of two species
which are just as devastating in their feeding habits and
which, like other mites, attack great numbers of plants.

The two-spotted spider mite is the species usually
called red spider; it feeds on nearly every greenhouse or
indoor plant, with ivies and roses being the most susceptible. Leaves turn completely gray or yellow or are smoth-
ered in fine, mealy cobwebs before dropping off. As the
mites are nearly microscopic, their webs are the first visible sign of an infestation. However, if this is your first
experience with mites, shake the foliage of the afflicted

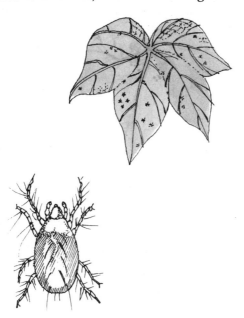

plant over a piece of white typing paper. If the tiny webs are actually mite webs and not cobwebs, you will be able to see the tiny spidery creatures crawling around on the paper. Also, tiny white flecks on the undersides of leaves might indicate mites; the flecks are shredded skins.

Both young and adult mites suck sap, puncturing leaf tissue and causing pale blotches, loss of color, and dry, rusty leaf textures. Unchecked, a mite infestation causes foliage to drop off completely before the plant finally dies.

Broad and cyclamen mites have habits that are different from those of other mites, and they are also noteworthy in that they are becoming two of the most prevalent and difficult-to-control plant pests. Both are microscopic, voracious feeders. An infestation of either pest prevents flowering if it occurs in spring, and if it occurs in late summer it causes distorted, blotchy bloom; stunted, twisted, or shriveled stems and leaves; dropping off of flower buds; and streaky, purplish foliage. These mites also cause chlorosis (see page 46), and their feeding produces wounds that promote the spread of bacterial and fungal diseases.

Because these mites favor cool temperatures and relatively high humidity, it is annoying to realize that if you correct growing conditions for other mites you may be producing quite favorable conditions for these particular ones.

Controls Spray forcefully and closely with cold water to dislodge mites and break down protective webs. Since these pests are the most difficult of all plant pests to eradicate and it is practically impossible to notice them until their damage to plants is relatively advanced, newly acquired plants should be isolated until you are quite certain there is no sign of a mite invasion. If you do detect mites on new plants or any other plant, do not handle healthy plants after touching infested ones without first washing your hands. Just a light touch with your fingers can spread mites from one plant to another.

Cedoflora, sprayed at weekly intervals with special attention to the underside of leaves and leaf axes, is a helpful preventive measure. Summer oils, such as Volck, or rotenone- or pyrethrum-based aerosol sprays, are fairly safe for the gardener and are reasonably effective miticides. Other products, such as Dimite, formulated especially for eradicating mites, are good, but the most effective controls are the systemic pesticides, such as Isotox or Systemic. Three applications at weekly intervals should eradicate even the worst infestation. Be sure to thoroughly spray the undersides of leaves and leaf axes.

If you cultivate a great many ivies and roses, you might find that to achieve any real control of mites you will have to apply Isotox or Systemic granules to the soil at regular intervals as a continuing preventive measure.

Plants affected   Palms, fuchsia, poinsettias, citrus, philodendrons, araucaria, aspidistra, maranta, dracaenas, spider plant, acuba, African violets and other gesneriads, cyclamen, cissus, geranium, annuals, herbs, ficus, aralia, smilax, and podocarpus. Ivies and roses are the most susceptible. In general, mites tend to feed on thin, papery-leaved, nonherbaceous and nonsucculent plants.

nematodes Nematodes are so numerous and destructive that an entire branch of botanical science called nematology has been devoted to their study. These microscopic wormlike creatures live and feed on root systems; they produce knots and galls on plant roots and eventually reduce an entire root system to a few gnarled stumps. Unfortunately, one cannot see the nematodes or their initial ravages until the damage has reached an advanced stage—the point where top growth has become weakened, sickly, or dwarfed. The damage is compounded by the fact that the wounds in the roots help the entry of root rots, fungi, and bacteria.

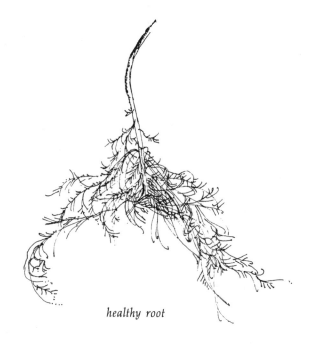

healthy root

Controls If you potted your plants in sterilized soil, you will probably never experience this pestilence. If you have not, and your plants are thus afflicted, soil, pots, tools, and even plant shelves must be sterilized. This very contagious pest can be spread around just by sticking your fingers

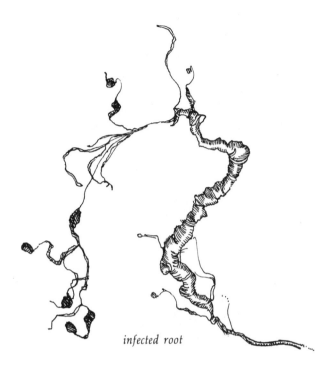

infected root

in an infested pot and then touching the soil of an uninfested pot.

Plants whose roots are badly chewed and gnarled and
whose top growth is already weakened should be destroyed. If some top growth is still sturdy, save it for cuttings, but pot the cuttings in a sterilized medium. Nematocides, such as V-C-13 are effective for mild infestations,
but follow the manufacturer's instructions for use on
specific plants. For plants that are particularly susceptible
one should give semiannual preventive treatments by
drenching the soil with V-C-13.

Plants affected   Crassula, geranium, hoya, columnea, African violets and other gesneriads, gardenia, citrus, *Ficus
decora*, podocarpus, palms. Look for plants grafted on ne-
matode-resistant stock if the problem seems to be particularly persistent.

slugs and snails Slugs are slimy, gray, inedible shell-less snails that usually appear at night; they leave shiny slime trails in their wake on any hard surface. Snails are the familiar mollusks that live in their own shells. Both chew on young, tender plant growth and hide themselves in daylight in moist gravel and on the bottom sides of flowerpots. Foliage chewed by slugs or snails is apt to look badly shredded.

Controls Inspect potted plants before you bring them into the house and remove and destroy slugs and snails. Keep growing areas clean and dry. If you still find these pests indoors in substantial numbers, put out a saucer of stale beer (leave the beer out overnight), which will attract snails and plain gray slugs. They will dive in for a taste and drown. Circling plants with sharp sand, lime, cinders, or fine crocking is a deterrent, because slugs and snails hate to crawl through anything gritty or irritating to their soft bodies.

Commercial metaldehyde-based soil drenches or slug baits are very effective controls but should not be used where house pets or children can get at them.

Plants affected Herbaceous (soft-tissued) plants, cacti and other succulents, and fleshy-textured plants.

Sowbugs are small gray pill-like creatures that are actually **sowbugs** terrestrial crustaceans (crabs and lobsters are marine crustaceans). The young feed voraciously on dead organic matter, tender stems and roots, and seedlings. They are usually seen clustered around the crowns of plants or swarming over the tops of pots.

Controls Hand-pick and destroy if you see even a few sowbugs. For a major infestation, spray Malathion on soil surfaces and/or drench the soil with V-C-13. Poison baits or ant and roach killers can be applied to soil surfaces, but do not wet foliage or leave baits where children and pets can reach them.

Plants affected Cacti and other succulents, fleshy-textured and tender growth, seedlings, and herbaceous (soft-tissued) annuals.

scale About twenty species of scale insects injure plant tissue by sucking sap from leaf and stem tissue and by secreting a sooty honeydew substance that coats leaves, attracts ants, prevents photosynthesis, and promotes fungus growth (see page 88). Scale appears on leaves and branches as small hard stationary disks that can be flicked off with a fingernail or picked off with tweezers. Soft scales do not have separate shells, and because they retain their larval legs, can move around. However, they move so slowly that they appear to be stationary. All species insert needlelike mouth parts into outer leaf and stem tissue and suck plant juices. Leaves then develop yellow spots or turn yellow altogether and finally drop off.

Controls Picking off scale can be a tedious but effective process if you work carefully and if the infestation is mild. Since ferns cannot be sprayed with anything except nicotine sulfate, hand-picking is the only solution for the first appearance of scale, but do not confuse the insects with fern spores. The spores are found on leaflets; the scale usually settles on the midribs of fern fronds. Systemic granules applied to soil provide further control and protection against scale for ferns.

Other plants can be sprayed with summer oils, such as Volck or Cedoflora, for mild infestations, but do not use summer oils on cacti. Malathion is probably the most effective control for major infestations. Use systemics or Malathion three times at weekly intervals.

Plants affected   Azalea, cacti, camellia, myrtle, crossandra, palms, ficus, aralia, bromeliads, citrus, ivy, hibiscus, ferns, euonymus, gardenia, pomegranate, oleander, ardisia, pittosporum, aspidistra, avocado, smilax, ligustrum, jessamine, Jerusalem cherry, schefflera, podocarpus, zamia.

Rx for Ailing House Plants

springtails These tiny jumping creatures are wingless and propel themselves by their tail-like appendages. Small round holes in thin-leaved plants, seedlings, and feeder roots might indicate the presence of springtails, which would otherwise usually be unnoticed because they hide in damp soil. However, a heavy watering can drive them up above the surface of the soil where you may notice them as specks of bright dark colors. Infestations are often provoked by overwatering (see pages 41–43).

Controls Correct watering habits if the problem seems persistent, and try growing plants on the dry side and keeping the growing area free of damp, decaying vegetation. Immersing pots in larger containers of water floods out the insects either to the top of the soil or into saucers from which they can be collected and disposed of. Drench the soil with Malathion or V–C–13 for stronger control, and use ant and roach spray on visible adults but do not wet the foliage.

Plants affected Seedlings and moisture-loving plants.

Thrips are small, flealike insects hardly wider than a sew- **thrips**
ing needle whose rasping, penetrating mouth parts scrape
and scar the undersides of smooth leaves and cause leaf
surfaces to become whitened and stippled, as in mite infestations. However, whereas mites are detected by their
webs, thrips leave tiny brown specks of excrement and
papery scars on leaves. Tips of new leaves become tightly
curled, and flower buds drop or are deformed and discolored if they do open.

Controls   Mild infestations can be treated by spraying
with lukewarm water, soapy water, or Cedoflora. Malathion sprayed especially on the undersides of leaves at
several weekly intervals is effective for controlling strong
infestations.

Plants affected   Any flowering ornamental, especially
roses, cinerarias, begonias, gloxinia, chrysanthemums,
fuchsia, azaleas, and cyclamen; aralia, *Ficus nitida*, myrtle,
avocado, Jerusalem cherry, asparagus ferns, and citrus.

Rx for Ailing House Plants

white If you shake leaves and clouds of snowflakes seem to fly
flies off, your plant has white flies. The tiny white adults are
always seen with tinier pale-green nymphs that look like
sesame seeds attached to the undersides of leaves. The
nymphs secrete a sticky honeydew that acts as a growing
medium for sooty mold (see page 88). Adults and nymphs
suck plant juices, causing foliage to turn yellow, or become
mottled or stippled, and finally die.

White flies are especially persistent and hard to get
rid of because contact insecticide sprays frequently miss
them as they fly around, and you can be sure that one or
two of them have managed to escape unnoticed to some
other plant.

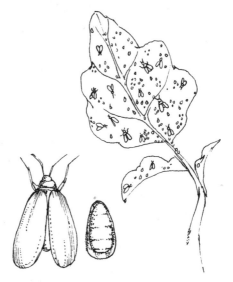

Controls Herbs, tomatoes, and other edible plants can be
dipped in buckets of soapy water, which should take care
of mild infestations. Malathion is probably safe to spray
on edibles for stronger control, because it has little residual
effect.

For other plants, systemic insecticides, such as Isotox
or Systemic, are the most effective controls. Either the

liquid or granular forms applied at three weekly intervals will render plants poisonous to these insects for weeks at a time, so that the white fly population will eventually be eliminated even if contact sprays do not catch them all.

For more immediate effect, enclose the plant in a plastic bag or cardboard carton and spray with an all-purpose or aerosol insect spray, but do not spray too close to the foliage. Leave the box or bag closed for several hours to allow the insecticide time to fumigate all the flies.

You might consider applying systemic granules to the soil every six weeks as a preventive measure if the problem seems to be persistent.

Plants affected Herbs, tomatoes, citrus, pomegranate, helxine, smilax, azalea, ferns, calceolaria, chrysanthemums, cineraria, coleus, geranium, hibiscus, Jerusalem cherry, browallia, pick-a-back, coffee plant, and annuals. Lantana and fuchsia are practically never without white flies; systemic applications are strongly advised as a preventive measure for these plants.

Chapter 5

Plant
Diseases

Under some unfavorable environmental conditions, live parasitic organisms develop that cause bacterial and fungal diseases on plants. Plant funguses are somewhat spongy-looking growths on plant tissue that resemble and are related to bread molds, mushrooms, and penicillin. They reproduce themselves from microscopic spores that germinate in conditions of excessive moisture or humidity. Bacteria are minuscule, single-celled organisms that function and reproduce only on living or dead organic food material. Insects, water, dirty tools or hands spread bacteria. Some bacteria serve as catalysts in certain beneficial natural processes, but others are parasitic types that feed on live plant tissue or animal tissue and cause such tissue to degenerate.

Extremely high or low temperatures, overwatering, very low light, excessive fertilizing, open wounds, air pollution, and too high humidity are the most common conditions that make plants susceptible to bacterial and fungal invasions.

anthracnose disease   A fungal disease, anthracnose is characterized by depressed leaf spots. The spots have dry centers, usually dark tan or black, and narrow dark margins. Sometimes the entire end of the leaf turns dark tan with darker bars crisscrossing the leaf. Anthracnose usually develops in very humid conditions but might also be caused by sudden chilling.

Controls   Destroy infected leaves and avoid misting until the disease is entirely cleared up. Plants so affected are responding to excessive moisture. Grow plants on the dry side at least until the disease clears up, and ventilate the growing area. Foliar fungicides such as Maneb, Ferbam, Zineb, or Bordeaux Mixture may be sprayed on remaining healthy leaves to ward off the spread of the disease.

Plants affected   Aglaonema, kalanchoe, citrus, ficus, oleander, palms.

These are fungal diseases that cause the stems and bases of affected plants to turn soft and mushy to the touch. Overwatering, excessive humidity, and extremely high or low temperatures produce these rotted surfaces, and the rots themselves spread rapidly throughout injured plant tissue.

crown and stem rot disease

Controls Cut out and destroy infected areas. Dust the wounds with such fungicides as Captan, Zineb, or Ferbam.

Plants affected Philodendron; African violet, gloxinia and other gesneriads, dieffenbachia, aglaonema, begonias, cacti and other succulents, geranium.

Rx for Ailing House Plants

damping-off disease Damping-off is a soil-borne fungus disease that mainly affects seedlings. The fungus attacks the lower portion of the stem which then collapses, causing leaves to turn inward and look pinched. Within a day or less, the seedling wilts and dies.

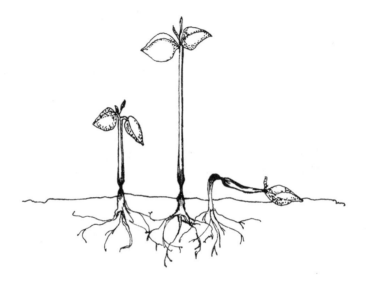

Controls Seeds should always be started in sterilized soil to prevent funguses from developing. At the first sign of wilting, reduce temperature, humidity, and watering. Apply fungicide dusts, such as Captan, for further control.

Plants affected Any seedlings, but especially those of herbaceous (soft-textured) plants.

Leaf spots might appear quite suddenly following physical **leaf spot** injury, or severe cultural or environmental deficiencies. **disease** The spots, usually yellow-margined with dark brown or black damp or blistered centers, are produced by bacterial or fungal invasions. High humidity, overwatering, chilling, low light, or poor ventilation are the most common causes. In severe infestations, the plant might defoliate entirely.

Controls Increase light, as well as temperature levels; ventilate the growing area; and allow soil to dry out before rewatering. Destroy all infected leaves. Spray foliar fungicides, such as Maneb, on remaining leaves, or try using a systemic fungicide, such as Benlate, for long-range control.

Plants affected Geraniums; African violets, gloxinias, and other gesneriads; cacti; dracaenas; ligustrum; roses.

Rx for Ailing House Plants

mildews and molds Black, sooty molds appearing on leaves as a black coating are usually associated with honeydew secreted by aphids, mealy bugs, and particularly scale. These develop mainly in very humid conditions but are not a disease parasite. However, anything that coats leaves—even dust—blocks out light needed for plant growth, and the insects, of course, must be eradicated for other reasons.

A gray or white mold resembling bread mold on the surface of the soil is usually caused by keeping the soil too wet or by overusing organic fertilizers. Moldy soil is a common problem in plastic pots, because these pots are nonporous, which reduces drying time. The mold itself, besides being unsightly, further reduces drying time, which may generate other problems associated with over-moist soil.

Mildews are parasitic organisms that appear as white or grayish feltlike coatings on foliage. Besides blocking out light, they eventually cause leaves to curl and shrivel up. Mildews are usually caused by high humidity or any condition that keeps foliage constantly damp. Outdoors, a long spell of humid weather might mildew plants, and indoors poorly ventilated terrarium plants become mildewed.

Controls Ventilation is particularly important as a preventive measure and as a control for all molds and mildews. Black, sooty molds should be wiped off leaves with soapy water or a summer oil solution, and suitable controls applied for aphid or scale pests.

Soil molds may be scratched gently into the soil, and watering should be reduced, particularly for plants in plastic pots. If the problem is persistent, drench soil with a dilute solution of Captan.

Lower humidity to control mildew. Mildewed leaves should be picked off and destroyed, and foliage and/or systemic fungicides applied for strong control or if the problem is fairly serious.

Plants affected Plants commonly host to aphids and scale insects; annuals, particularly the soft-leaved types; roses; ficus; and plants grown in plastic pots or in any damp environment.

root rot disease Funguses that invade plant roots diminish the roots' ability to absorb water. When this happens, top growth exhibits the typical signs of underwatering—that is, new growth dies back, the entire plant wilts, and finally the plant dies. Since the plant gives every indication of needing water, you may think that you must water it more frequently and in larger amounts. Unfortunately, this procedure will only intensify the problem.

Controls Remove affected plants from their pots; wash all old soil off roots under lukewarm tap water, and repot plants into fresh, sterilized soil. Water plants only often enough to keep them from seriously wilting, until they have completely recovered and have resumed normal growth. It is essential to drench the soil with a fungicide, such as Captan. If plant roots are completely rotted away, you can strike cuttings, but be sure to root them in a sterilized mix.

Plants affected   African violets, gloxinia, and other gesneriads; aloe, cacti, kalanchoe, and other succulents; begonias; palms.

Chapter **6**

Preventive Measures and Remedies

There are many steps you can take to prevent environmental, cultural, or parasitic plant problems, or if they should occur, as is sometimes inevitable, at least to mitigate the extent of the damage.

A growing environment—the light, temperature, and humidity of the growing area—that closely resembles the plant's native habitat encourages strong, healthy growth and reduces the possibility of environmental weaknesses conducive to the developing and spreading of disease and to infestation by insect organisms. Before acquiring new plants, find out what light exposures they grow best in or can adjust to, what nighttime and daytime temperature ranges are suitable, and whether their growing area should be fairly damp or relatively dry. If this information is unavailable, at least try to find out where the plant originates. Knowing its climatic and topographical origins should help you determine a plant's environmental requirements.

Cultural practices—soil mixing, watering, and fertilizing—should be specific to each plant, that is, as individual as the plants themselves, in order to ensure optimal plant health and strengthen resistance to disease and insect invasions. For example, a philodendron in a six-inch plastic pot ordinarily requires less frequent watering than a philodendron in a six-inch clay pot, because the soil in the plastic pot dries out much less quickly than the soil in the clay pot. A soil mixture that perfectly suits a well-grown dracaena may be too heavy-textured for a newly rooted dracaena cutting whose root system is delicate and relatively undeveloped. Fertilizing schedules shift with the changing seasons, but even two similar plants may require different fertilizing practices at a given time because one is growing faster than the other. Read the label for method of application.

Old soil and soil components may be saved for mixing with fresh new soil if the old soil is sterilized first. Sift out rocks and other debris; spread out the soil two inches deep in flat pans or pie plates, and bake in a 200-degree oven for three hours. Stir occasionally and allow it to stand for several days before using.

Sterilize or thoroughly scrub garden soil, woods soil, driftwood, beach pebbles, rocks—in short, any gardening materials brought in from outdoors that have not been purchased in packaged, presterilized form—because outdoor materials may be harboring disease organisms or insect eggs. People who find crickets hopping around in their homes at Christmastime can usually trace an invasion of these summer pests to a log or some moss in which summer insects frequently hibernate and lay eggs. Although these insects or eggs would ordinarily lie dormant until spring, they will resume their warm-weather life cycles much earlier in a heated household.

Good housekeeping—removing dead leaves, dust, and decaying organic matter from the growing area, the plants, tools and gardening accessories—is an important preventive measure. Many insects and several types of bacteria and funguses breed in decomposing vegetable matter, and once these parasites develop they will feed on your plants. Scrub old planters, pots, baskets, and jardinieres in hot soapy water and disinfect with Clorox (¼ cup Clorox per quart of water) before using them for new plants, especially if any of these containers were used for sick plants.

Mist weekly or twice weekly with lukewarm water to rid foliage of dust and soot particles, most insect eggs, and, often, the first few unnoticed insects that might later become a massive infestation. Spray leaf axes and undersides where most insects and their eggs tend to lodge. Large-leaved plants can be sponged off. Cedoflora, a mild summer oil, can be used as a stronger preventive measure; one teaspoon mixed with a pint of water makes an excellent solution for giving shine to the plants as well as providing a deterrent to pest infestation.

New plants sometimes falter a little while adjusting to their new environment, but when their cultural needs are met, they should revive in a week's time or less, if they are healthy plants. Whether you acquire the new plant from a fellow gardener or from a plant store, be sure to inspect it carefully for insect and disease symptoms before bringing it home. Isolate it for several days from your other plants until you are reasonably certain it is pest-free.

Plants that have summered outdoors or annuals dug up from the garden for winter bloom should be carefully inspected for signs of insects and treated accordingly *before* bringing them into the home. Be sure to take all plants out of their pots and look closely at the root systems without removing all the soil for traces of root- and soil-borne pests. (If your plants have grown vigorously, as they should have during their summer outdoors, you will probably have to take them out of their pots anyway for repotting.)

Wash your hands, gardening gloves, and all tools after working with infested plants or before touching healthy plants. If you have been handling someone else's plants, wash your hands before handling your own. Parasitic organisms are so minuscule that one cannot see them on one's own hands; the gardener can quite unwittingly spread insect eggs and disease organisms from one plant to another just by touching plants or using the same tools for healthy plants that have just been used on diseased plants.

Preventive spraying with hazardous chemicals is usually not recommended. Spraying with chemicals should be a specific response to a specific parasite, and the remedy used should be one that is recommended for that parasite. If nonchemical or cultural controls prove effective on any parasitic pest, use these methods. The one exceptional circumstance that might call for using chemical solutions as preventatives would be in the event of repeated infestations of particularly persistent pests. People who cultivate ivies or roses find that the preventive measures are necessary if they wish to have even minimal control of mite invasions on these plants.

types of controls Certain controls that operate very well in outdoor gardening will not work in indoor gardening. Indoor growing conditions do not lend themselves to a "balance of nature" for the simple reason that indoors is not nature. Natural controls—where local weather, topography, and insect predators keep plant predators in check—obviously do not exist in an indoor growing situation. Biological controls—introducing beneficial insects or other plant-pest predators—are also ineffective indoors, because there will never be enough indoor plant insects to feed a colony of beneficial insects, and if there were, the plants would be too ravaged at that stage to be worth saving. However, indoor gardeners have at their disposal three more types of controls: exclusion, nonchemical procedures, and the use of chemicals.

Control by Exclusion

For the indoor gardener, control by exclusion involves careful inspection of new plants *before* bringing them home to make sure they appear healthy and well-grown and have no apparent signs of insects or diseases. (See also preventive measures for new plants.) Some people enjoy reviving ailing plants, so they frequently accept discards from plant shops or friends. This practice is perfectly safe if you are prepared to totally isolate the ailing plants from your own healthy plants. If this is impossible or inconvenient, you take the enormous risk of infecting your own plants with whatever ailments the new, unhealthy plants are suffering from.

Nonchemical controls

Minimize the effects of disease or insect injury by responding promptly to the first symptom with a remedy specifically applicable to that problem. Careful observation of your plants (watering is a good time to take a close look at them) will reveal unnatural changes in appearance or growing habits.

Pick off and destroy soil-borne insects as soon as you see them. Usually you will notice them around the sides of pots and saucers or on top of the soil before they have a chance to lay eggs or feed on foliage.

Eradicate insects hiding in the soil by removing the plant from its pot, shaking all the soil gently off the roots, and washing the roots under a slow, lukewarm faucet. Repot the plant in fresh, sterilized soil in a fresh pot. Avoid

allowing the roots to dry out; if you do not repot immediately, enclose the roots in a plastic bag.

Dislodge foliage insects with a daily or twice-daily strong
spray of clear warm water or soapy water (use soap flakes,
not detergent). You risk dislodging leaves as well as the
insects, but if the leaves are that delicate, you may have
to resort to fine spraying with chemical remedies. If there
is no danger of damaging the leaves and if the insect infestation is mild, no further control other than the water
or soap spray should be necessary. But be sure to pick off
and destroy all dead or damaged leaves.

Discard very badly damaged plants.   A plant in the advanced stages of insect or disease infestation is not worth
saving. Its decaying top growth and/or root system encourages the development of additional parasitic organisms. If there are any parts of the plant that appear to be
uninfested, you may strike cuttings from them, after
spraying the cuttings to eradicate possible insect eggs.

A plant hospital—some room or window sill in your home
where ailing plants can be kept until they are fully recovered—is an effective means of keeping sick plants away
from healthy ones. The point cannot be too strongly made
that insect eggs and disease organisms are so easily spread
from plant to plant that what may begin as a mild invasion
of one or two plants may turn into a total devastation of
all your plants.

Chemical Controls

There are several basic types of insect and disease controls: broad-spectrum contact poisons, stomach poisons,
poison baits, fumigants, systemics, and drenches. Broad-
spectrum contact insecticides and fungicides are solutions
designed to kill a wide variety of organisms immediately

or shortly after they are sprayed with the solution. Stomach poisons are chemicals that are applied to foliage and will kill an insect when it sucks or chews on the leaves. Poison baits are small pellets of food mixed with toxic substances that attract insects and kill them when they eat the pellets. Fumigants are chemicals that kill parasites that breathe the vapors that rise around the area to which they are applied. Drenches are pesticide solutions poured into the soil; some act as fumigants and some as contact poisons. Systemics are chemicals absorbed through leaf or root tissue and transferred by the movement of plant juices to all parts of the plant. The plant itself becomes poisonous to insect predators, and because the systemic action lasts for weeks or even months, the plant has built-in protection for some time. Some particularly effective insecticide solutions are combinations of several pest-control chemicals.

Chemical controls of insects and plant diseases are now—and probably will be for years to come—a highly controversial subject. Many toxic substances have been removed from the marketplace, and no doubt more will be. Unfortunately, chemical controls are the most effective treatment for infestations of certain highly persistent pests at any stage and for others whose ravages have reached an advanced stage.

Certain precautions to take when using chemical remedies are worth observing, as no one will argue that a live gardener is to be preferred over any well plant or dead insect.

Follow manufacturers' instructions exactly for measurements of liquid concentrates, dosages per plant (sometimes depending on the size of the pot), expiration dates or length of time that solutions are viable and safe to use (for plants and gardeners), spraying distances, and frequency of treatments. Too strong a solution may kill the plant along with its predators and be harmful to the gardener, but too weak a solution is wasteful and ineffective.

Avoid inhaling spray solutions or splashing them on your face, skin, or clothing. Again, note the manufacturer's recommendations for personal safety. Skin and clothing contacted by chemicals should be washed thoroughly. Children, pets, and fishbowls should be kept somewhere else while spraying and until the spray has completely dissipated. Spray outdoors or in a well-ventilated room.

Do not ever suck or blow on siphons or tubes filled with toxic chemicals.

Leftover made-up solutions do not store well. Make up only as much concentrate dilution as you need at one time or dispose of the leftovers. Just as you would with medicines, store concentrate containers safely out of the reach of children and house pets and make sure containers are clearly labeled, tightly closed, and not exposed to strong light.

controls The following pesticides have proved to be effective controls, and when used as suggested here and on the container labels, are not harmful to the gardener. If the recommended solution or brand name is not available where you live, request a remedy that is as closely related as possible. Note that some pesticides are not recommended for use on edible plants, such as lettuce, tomatoes, and herbs.

Bulb dusts are contact insecticides and fungicides in powder form that kill a variety of insect and disease organisms when dusted on bulbs before planting or storing. Bulb Saver and Gladiolus & Bulb Dust are two effective brands.

Combination insecticides that act as broad-spectrum contact poisons, stomach poisons, and systemics include Isotox and Systemic. Isotox is composed of carbaryl (a contact insecticide also available as Sevin), methyl demeton (a systemic poison available as Meta-Systox) and kelthane (a miticide sold separately as Kelthane), and petroleum distillates. Systemic is formulated from methoxychlor (a contact insecticide, also available as Marlate), kelthane, methyl demeton, and petroleum distillates. Both Isotox and Systemic are liquid concentrates that can be used as sprays or drenches. Systemics are toxic by either skin or oral contact, but both products, used with care, are frequently extremely effective on mites, scale, and mealy bugs when nothing else will work. However, do not use them on edible plants.

Some plants are sensitive to contact insecticides. Ferns, lantana, verbena, and some gesneriads react negatively to the petroleum distillates used in most liquid solutions. Nicotine sulfate solutions or systemics applied to the soil may be better for these plants, but if in doubt, try a patch test on one or two leaves to see how the whole plant will react.

Fungicides are contact poisons designed to eradicate a variety of disease parasites or, in some cases, to prevent or alleviate symptoms of disease. Several good ones, available as liquid concentrates or wettable powders that are used as dusts or diluted with water, include Maneb, Ferbam, Zineb, Bordeaux Mixture, Captan (orthocide), sulfur (Flotox), benomyl (a systemic fungicide sold as Benlate).

Malathion is a broad-spectrum organic phosphate contact insecticide that is fairly nontoxic (except in extremely high dosages) to animals and humans and thus is one of the few pesticides acceptable at present to most environmentalists. Used as a spray or drench, it is a very effective control for a wide variety of insect pests infesting foliage, soil, the household, and even animals. It is sold as a 50 percent solution of Malathion or Cythion, a newer product said to be especially low-hazard. Some plants, especially ferns, cannot tolerate Malathion.

Metaldehyde is the principal chemical ingredient in a variety of products (Slug Killer, Slug-it, Slug and Snail Bait) that are used to attract slugs and snails, which die when they eat the bait. Some brands are formulated with calcium arsenate and should not be applied directly to the plants themselves.

Miticides include a variety of spray or drench contact insecticides especially formulated to kill mite eggs and/or mite adults. Formulations vary, so the manufacturer's instructions should be followed carefully for use on edible plants and for safety controls. Dimite (DMC) is particularly effective for eggs of all mites and can be used on gesneriads and other plants that are sensitive to other insecticides, but it should not be used on edible plants. Ovex, sold as Ovotran, and tedradifon, sold as Tedion, are effective miticides of very low toxicity to animals, humans, and plants.

Nematocides are contact or fumigant poisons used as soil drenches to eradicate such root and soil-borne pests as nematodes and earthworms. One product, V-C-13 Nemacide (a phosphate nematocide, contact poison, and miticide), is formulated with chlordane, an organic hydrocarbon that wipes out practically anything that crawls. However, as chlordane sold under that name is extremely toxic, V-C-13 is a safer alternative that can be sprayed around pots and saucers to control such crawlers as ants and sowbugs, and V-C-13 is an effective soil drench. Try a leaf-patch test first, as some plants are sensitive to various nematocides. Another product, Nemagon—also sold as Fumazone—is a fumigant nematocide that can be used safely around most plants.

Nicotine sulfate is a tobacco extract that is an old stand-by remedy for many plant pests. Currently sold as a 40 percent solution called Black Leaf 40, it is widely hailed as an organic (read "safe") pest control but is in fact an extremely toxic substance when inhaled or swallowed, or when it contacts the skin. However, it has little residual effect on edible plants and is an effective control for many foliage pests on plants whose tissues are damaged by other insecticides. The usual dosage is to mix one teaspoon of Black Leaf 40 with one ounce of soap flakes in a gallon of water. This solution may be used as a drench or spray.

Pyrethrum, a substance extracted from the dried flower heads of *Chrysanthemum cinerariaefolium,* and rotenone, a derivative of the plants Derris and Lonchocarpus spp., are contact and stomach insecticides that are the principal active ingredients in many all-purpose indoor and outdoor aerosol sprays. While not as effective as Isotox or Malathion, both substances have very low toxicity for humans and animals. Fishbowls, however, should be removed or covered while spraying. Rotenone is listed as such on container labels, but pyrethrum may be described by its active principles, pyrethrins I and II or cinerin I and II. Both types of aerosols may contain other products, such as piperonyl butoxide, but pure formulations (Tri-Excel DS, for example) are available. Do not inhale any more of the spray than you can help; aerosols tend to irritate the lungs and throat.

Roach and ant sprays, of which there are a variety sold in aerosol form, may also be used effectively on other crawling or jumping insects, such as crickets or springtails. However, most of these aerosols are formulated from such substances as naled (Dibrom) and Lindane that are highly toxic to humans and animals as well as to plant tissue. Spray only on soil surfaces (cover plants with plastic bags) and observe the manufacturer's instructions for safe usage.

Summer foliar oil sprays are petroleum-based products in emulsifiable and miscible oils that mix with water, are safe for the gardener, and are reasonably effective contact miticides, scalicides, and insecticides. Volck, composed of volck oil, and Cedoflora, a mixture of pine and hemlock oils, are harmless products except if swallowed. Cedoflora can be sprayed weekly on foliage as a preventive measure against mites, but no summer oil should be used on cacti or ferns.

Systemics formulated without other types of control action are available in dry granular form to be scratched into topsoil. These products contain small amounts of Di-Syston and, like the liquid systemics, are available under the brand names of Isotox and Systemic. Systemics, because they render all parts of the plant poisonous, cannot be used on edible plants but serve effectively as long-range preventive controls for scale, mites, and mealy bugs on ferns, lantana, and other plants whose tissues do not tolerate contact insecticides.

methods of applying pesticides There are several easy, practical methods of applying pesticide controls indoors that require minimal equipment and take very little time. You will need a plastic mister bottle—a hand-held, intermittent, atomizer-type sprayer that comes in pint and quart sizes with an adjustable nozzle; measuring spoons (be sure you have the one-eighth, one-fourth, and one-half teaspoon sizes); a measuring cup; a quart-sized glass jar; a watering can; plastic bags of various sizes; and flat pans or pie plates. All equipment should be reserved for use only with chemicals.

Sprays are dilutions of liquid concentrate pesticides, and applied with a mister bottle. Adjust the nozzle to a fine spray for better penetration of leaf tissue and fuller coverage of the infected areas. Do not spray in any hot, closed room or during hot, humid weather, because in such a situation the chemicals can cause leaf burn and general tissue disease. Manufacturers' instructions usually give spraying distances, but ordinarily about six to twelve inches is adequate for control. Spray in a well-ventilated area and away from your face. Work carefully toward thoroughly coating the undersides of leaves and leaf axes, where many insect pests are hiding.

Aerosol sprays are premixed, so they are easy to use, but recommendations for spraying distances must be followed religiously because the aerosol propellants and the excessively fine aerosol mist can easily freeze foliage and irritate lungs if inhaled. Be sure to follow the instructions on the label specifying the plants for which aerosol may be used; if there is any doubt, patch-test a few leaves.

One good method for aerosol spraying on all but the very largest plants is to cover the plant with a plastic bag and spray through the opening in the bag. Tie or tape the opening and leave it closed for a few hours.

Dips are sometimes recommended as a method for applying liquid solutions that is guaranteed to reach all parts of a plant. This involves immersing the plant sideways or upside down in a container filled with the pesticide solution that is large enough to contain most of the top growth. The soil must be covered with tin foil to keep it from falling out as you turn the plant over. Obviously, it is impractical to do this with large plants, but you may want to try it with small plants, particularly those with masses of tiny leaves, some of which might be difficult to reach with a spray.

Drenches are liquid or water-soluble powder concentrates mixed with water and poured into the soil. Use a clean glass jar for mixing dilutions and pour the mixture into your watering can. Water potted plants from the top or treat unpotted soil by spreading it out in flat pans and pouring the mixture over it.

Systemic granules are scratched into one or two inches of soil at the top (be sure not to disturb the feeder roots) in much the same manner as with dry fertilizer granules. Water the plant immediately afterward; repeated waterings will dissolve the granules throughout the soil and they will reach the plant's root system.